RUSSIA, THE ATOM
AND THE WEST

OTHER BOOKS BY GEORGE F. KENNAN

★

Russia Leaves the War
(Volume I of *Soviet-American Relations, 1917-1920*)

Realities of American Foreign Policy

American Diplomacy, 1900-1950

RUSSIA, THE ATOM AND THE WEST

by

GEORGE F. KENNAN

New York

HARPER & BROTHERS PUBLISHERS

Two articles based on Chapters III, IV, V, and VI appeared in the February and March, 1958, issues of *Harper's Magazine* under the titles, "A Chance to Withdraw Our Troops in Europe" and "How Can the West Recover?"

Library of Congress catalog card number: 58-8078

CONTENTS

FOREWORD

THESE TALKS were begun in the languor of a summer
holiday in Norway, by an author happily ignorant both of
the dramatic nature of the international atmosphere of the
forthcoming autumn in which they would be delivered and
of the attention they would attract on the part of a listen-
ing audience obviously thirsty for discussions of just this
nature. The result was they had to be thoroughly rewritten,
currently, as days for their respective delivery approached,
in the effort to make them responsive to the questions that
were on people's minds at the moment.

For anyone who has once worked in the relatively orderly
atmosphere of a governmental planning staff, profiting by
expert advice and dealing with questions to which he has
been able to give at least the major portion of his professional attention, there is a certain inhibition to be overcome
in speaking as an individual, from retirement, about matters
of which he only reads, most superficially, in the news-
papers. The same problem begins to emerge here which we
find in so many other questions of contemporary life: the
unavoidable gap between specialized knowledge and public

understanding. In consigning these lectures to the publisher I am acutely conscious that I have been talking about things concerning which I know very little. I have had to ask myself more than once whether I had any justification in speaking publicly about these things at all.

But I am reluctant to cross that crucial border beyond which one admits that foreign affairs are exclusively the province of the full-time professional, in which the views of the private citizen can have no value. Even if this were largely so, the admission of it would carry us into a new range of political realities for which neither our political systems nor our habits of thought are prepared. For the moment, at least, the citizen must still try to think, to have opinions and to express them when there are others who would like to listen.

There is, of course, not a single question touched on here with regard to which there are not today people in our governments who have knowledge far more ample and up to date. Beyond that, while the BBC has been the soul of tolerance, the radio speaker can never be wholly oblivious to the rigid limits of the radio half-hour: the division of subject matter into just so and so many segments of just such and such a length inevitably produces artificialities at one point or another.

For these reasons I can hold no brief for the soundness and adequacy of all that I have said. There will be parts of it that are ill informed, others that are ill conceived, still others that are incomplete. Least of all would I think of recommending these reflections to governments as a finished program for action. What I have tried to suggest here is not what governments should do but what they should think about. There is not a single element of these talks which ought not, before becoming a basis for government action, to be passed through that fine filter of study and refinement which only the responsible processes of government can provide.

The fact remains that when these lectures were begun the international situation had never looked darker; and never, it seemed to me, had the official and public discussion of international problems assumed a grimmer, more rigid or less promising form. If what I have said has served to loosen up the terms of this discussion, to draw attention to the area within which we are fighting our own fears and making things harder for ourselves than they need really be, and to give heart to people in their relation to a problem —namely, the atomic weapon in Soviet hands—which will never be solved otherwise than by the ability to look resolutely away at times from its purely military aspects, I shall be happy to accept, in all humility, the many detailed criticisms which I know they deserve.

GEORGE KENNAN

RUSSIA, THE ATOM
AND THE WEST

CHAPTER I.

Russia:
The Internal Scene

TEN YEARS ago I happened to write an article for the American quarterly *Foreign Affairs,* which came to be spoken of as the X-article, and received a good deal more attention at the hands of the press than I am sure it deserved. It was a discussion of the nature of the Soviet regime, and of the problem it posed for Western society.

In recent months many people have asked me how the same problem looks to me today, and whether I could still take the same reassuring view of the prospects for coping with it that I was able to take in 1947. This is a very big question, and I cannot treat it exhaustively in a series of brief talks—I can only touch on certain individual aspects of it. But the moment does seem propitious for such a discussion, and one may hope that even a few cursory reflections will be useful.

What I would like to talk about first is the internal Soviet scene and its implications for us.

Ten years ago, in writing the X-article, I was obliged

to draw attention to the handicaps that rested at that time on Soviet economic development: the enormity of the destruction suffered during the war; the physical and spiritual exhaustion of the Soviet people; the uneven development of the Soviet economy to date, and the sad state of Soviet agriculture.

Today I am free to confess that Soviet economic progress in these intervening years, in the face of all these handicaps, has surpassed anything I then thought possible. In the brief space of twelve years the Soviet people have succeeded not only in recovering from the devastations of the war, but in carrying forward a program of industrialization which has made Russia second only to the United States in industrial output generally, and about equal to her, we are told, in the production of military goods. The recent launching of the earth satellite has been only a dramatization, misleading in some respects, but perhaps revealing in others, of this impressive economic success.

While conceding to the Soviet leaders and the Soviet people all the respect they deserve for this achievement, we must be careful not to exaggerate its significance. This expansion of the Soviet economy has taken place at a time when the economies of other countries have also been expanding rapidly. During this same postwar period the growth in the productive capacity of my own country, for example, has probably actually been greater in absolute terms than that of Russia.

Now it is, of course, true that the comparative rate of growth in Russia from year to year has been greater than in the United States, and if these trends should be continued indefinitely the Russians would, eventually, catch up with us and outproduce us in many respects.

But actually I think it unlikely that the rate of growth of the Soviet economy will be maintained for long at the present level. Russia has been enjoying, up to this point, many of the possibilities for rapid growth that attend a relatively early stage of industrialization. But her economy is now coming into maturity. She is beginning to run up against problems, organizational problems, manpower problems, and others, which are familiar to all the advanced industrial countries. There is no evidence to date that she has better answers to these problems than any of the rest of us.

We must also remember that the general imbalance which has always characterized the development of the Soviet economy has not yet been fully overcome. Soviet economic progress has thus far represented in fact essentially the fulfillment of a program of military industrialization. Its success has been purchased at the cost of the serious neglect, and even exploitation, of other branches of the economy, as well as a continued repression of living standards. Agriculture, in particular, was shamefully neglected and abused throughout the Stalin era, and while Stalin's successors have indeed made efforts to overcome many of these abuses, some of us are not convinced that they have yet arrived at a correct analysis of the problem, or that they are prepared to do the things that would be necessary if they were to meet it. It remains to be demonstrated, in fact, that collectivization, as heretofore practiced in the Soviet Union, is really a feasible and hopeful manner of developing the agricultural resources of a great country. The experience of the satellite area would certainly not seem to indicate that it is. And even in the Soviet Union the collective farm system has now had to be supplemented by what we in America would call "the plowing up of the dust bowl"—a practice we are coming to recognize as short-sighted and undesirable.

Had a normal balance, or what we would consider a normal balance, been observed in the shaping of Russia's economic growth in these last two or three decades, I think it can well be questioned whether the development of its industrial sector alone would have been appreciably more rapid than that of other countries in a comparable stage of industrialization. It is often forgotten that even prior to the revolution Russian industry was already developing very rapidly, but under quite a different system and without the distortions and hardships that have attended its forced growth under Soviet power.

But when all of this is taken into account, the economic progress achieved by Russia in recent years does remain impressive; and I think that we must, barring unforeseeable accidents, expect it to continue into the future, though at a somewhat decreasing rate.

When we turn now to the political side of the internal Russian scene things are much more uncertain. Here two great problems present themselves. The first is that of the distribution of power among the members of the top group and the periodic transmission of it from one set of hands to another. The other is the satisfaction of the demands of the people below, and particularly of the academic youth and the cultural intelligentsia, for greater freedom of thought and expression. One, you see, is a problem of relationships within the top echelons of the regime; the other of relationships between the regime and the people.

The situation in the senior echelons of the regime is characterized at this time by the fact that the Communist party has been, in recent years, by no means the only channel of advancement to personal power and influence within the Soviet system. Industrial management, the armed services and, to some extent, science and engineering have provided careers in many ways more attractive than that of the regular apparatus of the party. Those external professional empires have been only loosely linked to the party through the membership of a few of their senior figures in the top policy-making bodies, the Presidium or the Central Committee.

In the period immediately following Stalin's death Khrushchev had no choice but to share power extensively with these outside entities as a means both of consolidating his personal position and of enabling the system to survive the shock occasioned by Stalin's death. More recently he has been trying to divest himself of this somewhat cloying partnership, to reassert the clear predominance of the party over all these professional elements and, at the same time, to strengthen his own position within the party. Were he to succeed in all this the result would, of course, be in many ways the re-establishment of a form of Stalinism, only minus, thus far at least, the terrorism of the secret police. Khrushchev has now been formally successful in a number of these efforts; the expulsion of Zhukov was only the last and the most important of them. But the success has been purchased at a heavy cost. There is a great deal more talent in Russia today outside the apparatus of the Communist party than inside it. Khrushchev has now offended and estranged from the central political process, one by one, the intelligentsia, the industrial managers and a portion of the officer corps of the armed services. He has now achieved the pinnacle of power which he apparently wanted, but I suspect that he is rather isolated up there and that the winds around him are becoming increasingly chilly. Plainly this is not a very stable situation, and it is hard to see how real stability can be achieved until some regular arrangement is made for the representation of these outside professional hierarchies in the key processes of government. But if this is done what becomes then of the traditional role of the party?

The Soviet leaders stand here at a parting of the ways. Either they keep up with the times and change the system, or they relapse into the rigidities of Stalinism at an ever-increasing cost to the ultimate soundness of the system itself.

The same sort of a dilemma, but even more marked, exists in the relationship between the regime and the people. A great deal has been written in these recent months about the restlessness of the Soviet intelligentsia and the student youth and about its causes. Many commentators have correctly pointed out that the Soviet Government is in this case the author of its own difficulties. By its admirable program of popular education—a program which also, in many ways, deserves our full respect—it has created a new educated class which is simply not prepared to accept the old devices of Communist thought control and is determined to do its thinking for itself. Here, as well as among the older figures of the Russian cultural world, there is now a powerful and in fact irrepressible demand for complete intellectual and cultural freedom.

Stalin's successors, thinking to undo some of the evil effects of his ruthless repression of intellectual and artistic activity, at first made moderate concessions to the feelings of the intellectuals, but the effect of these concessions was mainly to reveal the full depth of the unhappiness of these people and the startling degree to which the Marxist-Leninist ideology had lost its power over their minds and their creative impulses. Frightened at what they saw, the leaders have recently drawn back and have made a fumbling effort to reimpose something like the old Stalinist controls over cultural life. But surely this is no adequate response. It is already too late to recapture minds which have once begun to ask troubled and penetrating questions. If the leaders attempt to go further along the road of repression they are only going to alienate the intelligentsia entirely and lose its indispensable co-operation in maintaining the morale and the enthusiasm of the people at large. If, on the other hand, they go further in the attempt to meet the real needs of the educated strata of the people —and in increasing measure these are the needs of the people at large—then I am sure they will find no stopping point short of complete cultural freedom, and whether this is compatible with Communist rule is something to which the Communists themselves have, on many occasions, given a negative answer.

The pattern which we are obliged to discern then on the Russian internal scene is a mixed one. Economic progress, yes, but against a background of deepening crisis on the political front, crisis in the relationship of the senior figures to each other, crisis in their relationship to the people over whom they rule, slow crisis, to be sure, in the latter case, not likely to come to a head tomorrow, but serious and logical crisis, not readily to be resolved by anything short of complete cultural and political freedom.

Now what does this pattern of internal realities in Russia mean for us here in the West? Let us take first the economic advance. The Soviet Government has, of course, lost no occasion to exploit this sort of achievement for political purposes. It has endeavored at every turn to present itself as participating in an all-out competition with the Western countries for industrial growth and then to interpret every element of its economic progress as a triumph for its own system of economy and a defeat for the Western world. A great many people in my own country, perhaps elsewhere as well, have come unconsciously to accept this Soviet thesis, to believe that every Soviet gain is automatically our loss and to see our salvation as dependent on our ability to outpace Russia in every single phase of her economic progress.

I am bound to say that I cannot see it this way at all. There's nothing unnatural in the fact that Russia is now rapidly industrializing. Her development in past centuries has lagged behind that of the Western peoples; she has a large and vigorous population, rich in talents of every sort; she occupies a territory liberally endowed with the resources which permit successful industrialization everywhere. If, given these facts and the spirit of the modern age, the Russian people were not now rapidly industrializing their country, this, rather than what is occurring today, would be the true wonder.

I cannot find it in my heart to begrudge the Russians this kind of success; nor can I see that we are in any way handicapped by it in our attack on our own problems. If the

Soviet Government loves to portray itself as embarked on a desperate economic competition with us, I don't see that we are under any obligation to accept this interpretation. One sometimes has the impression that Mr. Khrushchev sees international life as one great sporting event, where they and we contend for goals which they, not we, have defined, and where the world looks on.

Not a day passes, for example, but what the Soviet press summons the Russian people to catch up with and surpass America in the per capita production of meat, milk and butter. I simply cannot concede that we're engaged in any such competition. We in the United States have enough of these things. Our problem is not to produce more of them. I should hope that the Russian people, too, would soon have all they need of these and other articles of consumption. And whether this is more or less than our per capita production of them seems to me supremely unimportant.

When they do reach this point, I think they're going to discover—as some of us are now discovering—that this is not the final solution to all things, that the most serious problems in modern life only begin with the achievement of material plenty.

When I think of the enthusiasm of people in Moscow today for economic development, it puts me in mind of my own youth in the American Middle West, and of the inordinate pleasure many of us used to take in the headlong economic progress of that region. We Americans were known as the "Babbitts" of the early twentieth century, and I suppose we were. But many of us, at least, became conscious of the shallowness of this outlook, and it was, after all, an American who coined the word for it. The Russians are now the "Babbitts" of the mid-century. But so far, being good materialists, they have shown no awareness of the limitations of this outlook.

It will be a happy day for everyone when they, too, have solved their problems of production, and can join us in grappling with some of the deeper, more subtle, and more significant problems that lie at the end, rather than at the beginning, of the economic rainbow.

Many of my countrymen would reply to these observations by saying: "What you say is all very well, but how about the military aspects of Soviet economic progress? Do they not spell for us the deepest and most terrible sort of danger?" I hope, later on, to be able to speak in greater detail about this military problem. Let me only say at this point that I fail again to understand the frame of mind that sees in every evidence of Soviet economic or scientific progress some new deterioration in Western security. One is moved to wonder, sometimes, how long it will be before people can bring themselves to realize that the ability to wreak terrible destruction on other peoples now rests in a fairly large number of hands in this world, and that the danger is already so great that variations in degree do not have much meaning.

I am not particularly concerned to learn whether our

Soviet friends could, if they wished, destroy us seven times over or only four times; nor do I think that the answer to this danger lies in the indefinite multiplication of our own ability to do fearful injury to them. Our problem is no longer to prevent people from acquiring the ability to destroy us—it is too late for that. Our problem is to see that they do not have the will or the incentive to do it. For this, of course, we have to preserve and cultivate our deterrent capacity. But that is a limited task, not an unlimited one, and it does not necessarily imply an endless industrial and scientific race against the Russians.

Again it will be argued by anxious people, "Yes, but if the Russians gain on us in the race for economic development, the peoples of the underdeveloped areas of the world will come to look to them, rather than to us, for economic guidance, and then, where shall we be?" This, too, is something about which I shall have some things to say on another occasion.

Suffice it to observe here that it strikes me as a dangerous thing for us to assume that our security must depend indefinitely on keeping the Russians from shouldering their part of the responsibility all industrialized nations bear for giving this sort of aid and guidance to the underdeveloped ones. People have things to learn from Russia, I am sure, as well as from us; there will be many ways in which our economic system, based as it is on the specifics of our legal and commercial tradition, will not be fully relevant to the problems of people elsewhere, and where the Russians may have more to offer than we do. But the same is going to be true conversely. These things must be permitted to find their own level, and when they do I am sure there will be no lack of opportunity and of work for all of us.

The fact is that we in the West are, of course, engaged in a competition with Russia, but it is not the kind of competition the Russians claim it is; we are not pursuing the same objectives, we are not at the same stage of development, our tasks are not similar. The real competition is rather to see which of us moves most rapidly and successfully to the solution of his own particular problems, and to the fulfillment of his own peculiar ideals. To my own countrymen, who have often asked me where best to apply the hand to counter the Soviet threat, I have accordingly had to reply: to our own American failings, to the things that we are ashamed of in our own eyes, or that worry us. To the racial problem, to the conditions in our big cities, to the problems of education and environment for our young people; to the growing gap between specialized knowledge and popular understanding in our country. I imagine that similar answers could be found for any of the other Western countries.

And I would like to add that these are problems which are not going to be solved by anything we or anyone else does in the stratosphere. If solutions are going to be found for these problems it is going to be right here on this familiar earth in the dealings among men and in the moral struggle within the individual human breast. If one had to choose between launching satellites and continuing to give attention to these more homely problems here below, I should a hundred times over choose the latter, for unless we make this sort of progress in our problems on this earth no satellite will ever save us. Whether we win against the Russians is primarily a question of whether we win against ourselves.

So much for our reaction to the economic progress in Russia. There are converse dangers to be guarded against in our reaction to the political dilemmas with which the Soviet leaders are now confronted. Since their problems are not our problems we will do well not to claim triumph from every one of their reverses. We have ourselves not found perfect solutions to the questions of political life in the industrial age. But beyond this, let us not forget that the happiness of the peoples under Soviet rule is also involved in the solution of these problems. There is a certain intimacy between the fortunes of rulers and ruled, even in the curious relationships of the authoritarian state. And I for one could wish, in the interests of the Russian people, that Russia's progress toward more mature political institutions might proceed with as little violence and trouble as possible —not with as much.

My plea, then, is for greater detachment and reservation of judgment on our part toward internal happenings in Russia. Their world is not our world; their fortunes need not always be the diametrical opposite of our own; we have reason neither to quake before the spectacle of Soviet economic progress, nor to crow over the fact that the Soviet Government faces political dilemmas at home. Our problem is rather with the external behavior of the Soviet leaders, and it is to this that I shall turn in the next of these talks.

CHAPTER II.

The Soviet Mind
and World Realities

IN THE previous talk I discussed internal developments in the Soviet Union. In this one it is the external attitudes of the Soviet leaders that I should like to speak about, and particularly the psychological background of their reactions in foreign affairs.

We are all familiar with the posture of irreconcilable hostility, ostensibly only toward the Western governments but in effect toward the Western peoples as well, which has at all times animated the Soviet leaders. We have learned to expect at their hands an unremitting effort to undermine our world position, to disrupt our relations with those who have formerly been our friends, to destroy our confidence in ourselves and the confidence of others in us, to reduce us, in short, to a state of isolation, helplessness and impotence in the affairs of the world.

Now what is it that could bring men to take so intolerant and unpromising an attitude, one so out of accord with the obvious needs of our time, and so sure to produce tensions, dangers and inconveniences for themselves as well as for everyone else? I think one must clarify one's answer to this question before one can think usefully about the Western response.

The rationale for this posture on the part of the Soviet Government has, as we all know, invariably been expressed in ideological terms—in the characteristic jargon, that is, of Marxist-Leninist thought. There has been a common tendency here in the West in recent years to dismiss this ideological posture as mere window dressing, to ignore its political content and implications, and to see behind it nothing more than a primitive lust for military conquest— usually envisaged as a determination to overrun Western Europe, in particular, by force of arms, as soon as military conditions might prove favorable.

I personally feel that this is a dangerously inaccurate view of what we are up against and I believe many others who have known Russian Communism at first hand would feel the same. The hostility has been there, certainly; and it has been a deadly hostility, aimed at a destruction of all that we most intimately cherish—a destruction no less sweeping, no less final than that which would be occasioned by an outright war. But the threat has not been one of all-out military attack. It has been a combined political and military threat, but more political than military—a threat intimately associated with the weaknesses of our Western civilization itself—looking to these weaknesses, in fact, rather than to the strength of the Soviet arms, to constitute the main instruments of our undoing. The Soviet design has consisted, in other words, primarily of a determination to exploit every element of disunity, of confusion, of short-sightedness in our society, with a view to causing us to eliminate ourselves as rivals to Soviet power and influence everywhere.

Now in connection with this design armed force has, to be sure, been cultivated on a major scale by the Soviet Government. It has been cultivated partly as a precaution, partly as a psychological weapon, partly because it was always envisaged that the Soviet armed forces might someday be called upon to play a subsidiary role in the final phases of the demise of Western capitalism. But it has never—at least not until very recently—been looked to as the major instrument by which our undoing was to be accomplished.

One of the most serious evils of this overmilitarization of thinking in the West on the nature of the Soviet threat has been that it has confused people badly about the question of what could be done to meet this threat. Assuming that the ideological foundation for Soviet policy was simply disin-genuous, many people have tended to suppose either that the Soviet leaders were genuinely suspicious of Western purposes, and that this was the real cause of their hostility; or that they were simply evil men, who wanted power for its own sake and believed that they could outpace us in the military competition to a point where we could safely be attacked and disposed of. And taking one or the other of these views, people assumed that if only we could prove ourselves strong enough to discourage military aggression, or, correspondingly, if we could lay to rest the Soviet suspicions about our motives, this whole situation could be suddenly cleared up—an entirely new outlook could suddenly be induced in the Soviet mind—and the cold war would be terminated at a stroke. And as the culmination of this happy process, people usually envisaged some sort of a summit meeting, at which the last misunderstandings would be removed and agreements would be arrived at for a peaceful collaboration in the future.

In this manner, as you see, an oversimplified and over-militarized view of the cold war contrived to settle down quite comfortably, in many minds, beside a highly utopian concept of the ways in which this cold war could be brought to an end.

These tendencies naturally received a certain fillip in recent years from the death of Stalin. His successors appeared to be men of greater moderation and good-will and even humanity; and in some respects they really were—and are. Stalin, of course, also talked peace in his day, as Khrushchev does now; but he accompanied that talk with policies so harsh, so forbidding, so obviously imbued with a total enmity toward the Western world that even the most sanguine of us here in the West found it hard, in the end, to believe in the possibility of any amicable settlement. Stalin's successors, and especially Mr. Khrushchev, have talked peace with a greater show of warmth and earnestness; and they even accompanied this talk, initially, with just enough in the way of normalization of the atmosphere of Soviet diplomacy to lead many people to hope that perhaps things really had changed.

We have now had four years in which to study the political personality of this post-Stalin regime; and I am afraid that the time has come when we can no longer comfort ourselves with any of these illusions. Recent events, in particular, have left us no choice but to have a searching look at some of the peculiarities of the Russian Communist mind and to draw unsparingly the consequences of what we see.

From the time of their seizure of power, forty years ago, the Russian Communists have always been characterized by their extraordinary ability to cultivate falsehood as a deliberate weapon of policy. They began by adopting an attitude of complete cynicism about objective truth, denying its value if not its existence, declaring the lie to be no less useful and respectable than the truth if only it served the purposes of the party. Departing from this premise, they have systematically employed falsehood not just as a means of deceiving others and exploiting their credulity, but also as a means of comforting and reassuring themselves. It has seemed to them at all times easier, and in no way improper, to operate a militant political movement on the basis of convenient falsehood than on the basis of awkward truth.

I think we have to recognize today, particularly on the example of Khrushchev's recent statements and policies, that the effects of this systematic abuse of the human intellect are deep-seated and troublesome. Forty years of intellectual opportunism have wrought a strange corruption of the Communist mind, rendering it incapable of distinguishing sharply between fact and fiction in a single segment of its experience, namely in its relationship to any external competitive power. Let me stress that it is only in this one sector that the Communist mind is thus affected. In other respects, it is extremely shrewd and discerning.

I have been asked hundreds of times in recent years how it could be that men of such great native intelligence as the Soviet leaders, commanding so elaborate and costly a network of intelligence-gathering agencies, could be anything else but excellently informed about ourselves and everything having to do with us. I should like to suggest an answer to this question.

In everything that can be statistically expressed—expressed, that is, in such a way as not to imply any judgment on our motivation—I believe the Soviet Government to be excellently informed about us. I am sure that their information on the development of our economies, on the state of our military preparations, on our scientific progress, etc., is absolutely first-rate. But when it comes to the analysis of our motives, to the things that make our life tick as it does, I think this whole great system of intelligence-gathering breaks down seriously. It breaks down because over all these forty years the Communist party has made it impossible for the people who collect the factual information to accompany that information with any really objective analysis of the nature of Western society. Some of the fictions dearest and most basic to Russian Communism's view of itself would be jeopardized at every turn by that sort of analysis. The Soviet diplomatic representative or journalist abroad has no choice but to cast his analytical report in the terms of Marxist-Leninist ideology whether this is applicable or not in the given instance. In this way the Soviet leaders find themselves committed to a badly distorted image of the outside world.

Being thus committed, they are able to apprehend everything about us but the main things. They view us as one might view the inhabitants of another planet through a very powerful telescope. Everything is visible; one sees in the greatest detail the strange beings of that other world going about their daily business; one can even discern the nature of their undertakings; but what one does not see and cannot see is the motivation that drives them on these various pursuits. This remains concealed; and thus the entire image, clear and intelligible in detail, becomes incomprehensible in its totality.

The fact is that the Soviet leaders are the first and leading victims of the abuse they have practiced for so long on the freedom of the mind. I would not wish to maintain that they believe everything they say; I am sure they do not. But I would submit that their habitual carelessness about the truth has tended to obliterate in their minds the distinction between what they do believe and what they merely find it convenient to say.

It would be easier for us if they either believed things entirely or spoke them in utter cynicism. In either case, we would know where we stood. As it is, our problem is very difficult indeed; for we can never know, when we encounter their statements and reactions, whether we have to do with the substructure of sincerely held error which does indeed exist in their minds, or with the superstructure of contrived and deliberately cultivated untruth to which they are so committed.

Now, this, it seems to me, is what we are up against in the mentality of Mr. Khrushchev and his associates; and the implications for Western statesmanship are numerous and far-reaching. Let me mention only a few of those that seem to me of greatest importance.

We must accept, first of all, the fact that there is nothing anyone can do in any short space of time to alter this situation, to correct this corruption of thought, to make out of the Soviet leaders men capable of seeing world realities as we do. It is no good trying to argue them round to our point of view on any one occasion. They are men who can be directly influenced by situations, but not by words expressed in any terminology other than their own. There is nothing that can be said to Mr. Khrushchev on any one occasion by any Western figures, however illustrious, that would suddenly dispel this obscurity of vision. What we are confronted with here is not just misunderstanding, not just honest error, but a habit of the mind, an induced state, a condition. Even assuming for the sake of argument that it were possible to explain away in some satisfactory manner all the sources of misunderstanding and suspicion that prevail today between the Kremlin and ourselves, and to start all over again with a fresh slate tomorrow morning, I would still hazard the guess that twenty-four hours would not elapse before that fresh slate would be fouled with new misunderstandings, and precisely as a consequence of the congenital inability of our Soviet friends to see themselves and us and our mutual relationship with any proper degree of realism.

In the face of this situation, I wonder about the wisdom of engaging the persons of the senior Western statesmen directly in the process of negotiation with the Soviet Government. With people whose state of mind is what I have just described no intimacy of understanding is really possible. There is only one sort of thing that can usefully be said to them and that is: what we would be prepared to do, and what we would not be prepared to do, in specific contingencies. This sort of thing they understand; but to say it, you do not need the physical presence of a president or a prime minister; and there are even reasons why it is better not to have it. I would not wish to say that there is never a time for summit meetings. There is a time for almost everything in the strange world of diplomacy. But surely, if the usefulness of these senior figures is to be protected and the raising of false hopes avoided, such meetings should occur, if at all, at the end of the negotiating process, and for the purpose of formalizing agreements already arrived at, rather than at the beginning and as a means of starting the wearisome process of accommodation.

However one strives to disclaim the intention, meetings at the summit will never fail to suggest to the public mind the possibility of early global solutions—sweeping and spectacular solutions—to outstanding problems.

But it is precisely this possibility of such solutions that is ruled out by what we know of the condition of mind of the Soviet leaders. The road to a safer and more hopeful state of world affairs is not to be traversed in any "giant strides." On the contrary, if the tension between Russia and the Western world is to be reduced, it must be broken down into its individual components—into a number of specific problems, that is; and each of these must be treated empirically and on its merits with a view to arriving at those compromises and accommodations that would be least unsettling to world peace. And for this, it is not the hectic encounters of senior statesmen under the spotlight of publicity which we need; it is the patient, quiet, orderly use of the regular channels of private communication between governments, as they have grown up and proved their worth over the course of the centuries.

This implies, it seems to me, that we must discard our recent fear of bilateral communication and our attachment to the idea of negotiating with Russia only as a coalition. There has recently been a good deal of talk about strengthening the decision-taking process in NATO. Certainly we need the maximum real political intimacy within NATO. But we will be creating difficulties for ourselves if we over-formalize in any way the processes for discussion and agreement among us. Aside from the fact that we do have real differences within the NATO family in fields aside from Russian policy—deep, unavoidable differences, not to be bridged by creation of any new machinery—I fear for the effect on our relation to Russia if we make the procedures of NATO any more elaborate and more restricting than they are now. The delicate explorations and discussions which must precede accommodation in complex international questions cannot be conducted by a coalition, operating on the basis of sporadic, unanimous and highly formalized decisions. For this, you need the privacy, the authority and the day-to-day flexibility which only the sovereign government can provide. I would hazard the prediction that no solution to any serious problem of Soviet-Western relations is going to be discovered in meetings where a group of Western representatives, bound by prior understandings among themselves and limited by each other's inhibitions, confront the Soviet negotiators over a large green table, while the representatives of the world press wait in the next room to be briefed at once on all that has been said. We have urgent need to loosen up these rigidities of communication, to divest ourselves of the fear of all that is informal and exploratory, and to restore the element of privacy to the composition of differences.

In this same connection, I find myself worried at the frequent sight of the United Nations being involved in the issues of our conflict with Soviet power, and particularly the United Nations Assembly. Some of the most important elements in the East-West conflict long predated the foundation of the United Nations; they were part of the world into which it was born. It is not fair to the organization today to ask it to resolve the predicaments of the past as well as of the present. No international organization can be stronger than the structure of relationships among the Great Powers that underlies it; and to look to such an organization to resolve deep-seated conflicts of interest among those Great Powers is to ignore its limitations and to jeopardize its usefulness in other fields.

When I said, as I said a moment ago, that the Soviet leaders can be influenced by situations, I had in mind real situations, not parliamentary ones. The Soviet Government is not insensitive to deeper trends of world opinion, but it cannot easily be shamed into doing things or not doing them by the votes of international majorities. Soviet power, always addressing itself to peoples over the heads of their rulers, grew great on the defiance of the opinions of other governments; and it is not afraid today of votes in its disfavor. Not only will international majorities not be effective in modifying Soviet behavior but they may easily, as things now stand, be turned at any time against us in the West; and we, with our more legalistic tradition and our great moral commitment to the principle of international organization, will find it harder to defy them than the Soviets.

Many people, again, would like to by-pass the political issues entirely by agreements for general disarmament, and the effort to work something out along this line has recently preoccupied the attention of our governments and of the world public. I have great sympathy for the motives of those who have worked so hard to bring this dream to fruition; but I cannot agree that the approach is a very promising one.

It is true that armaments can and do constitute a source of tension in themselves. But they are not self-engendering. No one maintains them just for the love of it. They are conditioned at bottom by political differences and rivalries. To attempt to remove the armaments before removing these substantive conflicts of interest is to put the cart before the horse. At every turn, we are confronted with the fact that there is no way of evading those specific political problems —for the main part territorial questions, questions of who is to rule whom, and where and when—in which all this tension and trouble have their real origins. Only when these are alleviated, will the prospects for disarmament become real; and only then will all this painstaking preparatory work yield its dividends.

Let me return for a moment to the systematic Soviet distortion of the realities of our world and of the purposes to which we are dedicated. I should like to say that I think we cannot simply ignore this sort of thing. It is a serious error to dismiss Soviet falsehoods as "just propaganda" and to profess to find them too absurd and unimportant to answer. I am always startled at this phrase "just propaganda." Why "just"? What is the matter with propaganda? Is it not a serious and important force in world affairs? Let us not forget that these fantastic allegations are partially believed by those who say them, and they will be at least partially believed by many of those who listen. A wise Western policy will insist that no single falsehood or distortion from the Soviet side should ever go unanswered.

This will be tiresome. We do not like repetition. But we cannot afford to dispense with it. Truth does not win over error just on its merits. It, too, has to be assiduously propagated. I have asserted that there is nothing that could be said to the Soviet leaders in the space of a few days that would change their strangely corrupted mentality. But there are things which could be said to them every day over the course of several years, which would exert a useful discipline upon them, would make it harder for them to ignore the distinction between the real and the unreal, and would place limitations—thus far not visible—on their use of falsehood as a weapon of political policy.

All in all, then, I fear it is a comfortless message with which I have come before you. One by one I have felt obliged to bring into question all those devices to which the minds of people here in the West have most hopefully turned in these recent years: summit meetings, global solutions, coalition diplomacy, the United Nations, disarmament. And in their place I have suggested only the unglamorous devices of an informational war of indefinite duration, and a quiet old-fashioned diplomatic attack on certain of the individual political problems that divide us from the Soviet world. And having said this, I shall certainly be asked to explain what I consider these problems to be, and what I mean when I say that we should apply ourselves to their solution.

In my next talk, therefore, I shall venture to discuss that political issue which seems to me to be of greatest urgency and importance and the discussion of which encounters the deepest inhibitions on our part, and that is the problem of the future of Central and Eastern Europe.

But there is just one more thing I should like to mention.

What I have had to say about the Soviet relationship to the Western world has been based on the general pattern of Soviet behavior over these past few years. In recent weeks we have seen some things that do not entirely fit into this pattern. In particular the irresponsible, deliberate aggravation of Turkish-Syrian differences by people in Moscow strikes me as the most disturbing manifestation of Soviet behavior we have seen since the Berlin blockade.

Now I do not think that this changes the validity of what I have said earlier. I still see no reason to suppose that Moscow wants a general war. The main object of this extraordinary maneuver seems only to have been to drive a wedge, if possible, between Turkey and the United States, on the one hand, and the remainder of the NATO community, on the other. Possibly elation over the launching of the satellite has caused a momentary dizziness in Moscow; possibly domestic-political complications have also had something to do with it.

The fact remains that the Kremlin has recently shown itself more inclined to play close to the edge of serious international complications than at any other time in recent years.

To my mind, this only heightens the urgency of a careful re-examination of Western positions in our differences with Moscow. At such a time it is more important than ever that our posture should contain nothing that is unsound or superfluous, and should omit nothing which bears any hopeful and constructive implications for the future.

CHAPTER III.

The Problem
of Eastern and Central Europe

I REFERRED in the last talk to the specific issues involved in the relationship between the Soviet Union and the West.

These issues fall generally into two categories: the basic ones, by which I mean disagreements over things such as frontiers and the political control of territory, and the secondary ones—ones flowing, in this case, from the military rivalry that has now grown up between NATO and the Soviet bloc. It is the basic ones—and one of them in particular—that I want to talk about now.

I would know of no basic issues of genuine gravity between Russia and the West other than those arising directly from the manner in which the recent world war was allowed to come to an end. I am referring here particularly to the fact that the authority of a united German government was expunged on the territory of Germany itself and throughout large areas of Eastern Europe, and the armies of the Soviet Union and the Western democracies were permitted to meet in the middle of this territory and to take control of it, before there was any adequate agreement among them as to its future permanent status. This was, of course, the combined result of the unconditional surrender policy, which relieved the Germans of all responsibility for the future status of this area, and the failure of the Allied governments to arrive at any realistic understandings among themselves about it while the war was on. Since it has not been possible to reach such understandings subsequently, except in the case of Austria, the provisorium flowing from these circumstances has endured. It is this that we are faced with today.

There is, of course, a similar problem in the Far East. A precisely analogous situation prevails in the case of Korea and Formosa. The Allies dislodged the Japanese from these areas without having arrived at any proper understanding with the Russians as to their future status. There, too, the question remains open; and it does indeed constitute an issue in the relations between the Soviet Union and a portion of the Western community.

For reasons of time, and of simplicity, I shall restrict myself here to the European theater, though much of what I shall have to say would have its applicability to this situation in the Far East as well. In Europe, the difficulty obviously breaks down into two parts: the satellite area and Germany.

I am sure there is no need for me to go into detail about

the situation in the satellite area. Everyone knows what has happened in these past three or four years. The Moscow leaders made an attempt to undo some of the harm that Stalin had done with his policies of ruthless political oppression and economic exploitation. The first effect of this relaxation, as shown in the disorders in Eastern Germany and Poland and later in Hungary, was not to reconcile people to the fact of Soviet rule but rather to reveal the real depths of their restlessness and the extent to which the postwar arrangements had outworn whatever usefulness they might once have had. The Soviet leaders, startled and alarmed by these revelations, have now seen no alternative, in the interests of their own political and military security, but to reimpose sharp limits to the movement for greater independence in these countries, and to rely for the enforcement of these restrictions on the naked use or presence of their own troops.

The result has been, as we all know, the creation of an extremely precarious situation. It is a dangerous and unsatisfactory situation from everyone's standpoint. The state of the satellite area today, and particularly of Poland, is neither fish nor fowl, neither complete Stalinist domination nor real independence. Things cannot be expected to remain this way for long. There must either be further violent efforts by people in that area to take things into their own hands and to achieve independence by their own means, or there must be the beginning of some process of real adjustment to the fact of Soviet domination. In the first of these contingencies, we in the West could easily be placed once more before the dilemma which faced us last year at the time of the Hungarian uprising; and anyone who has the faintest concern for the stability of the world situation must fervently pray that this will not happen.

As for the second alternative, which at this moment seems to be the more likely of the two, it seems no less appalling. If things go on as they are today, there will simply have to be some sort of adjustment on the part of the peoples of Eastern Europe, even if it is one that takes the form of general despair, apathy, demoralization and the deepest sort of disillusionment with the West. The failure of the recent popular uprisings to shake the Soviet military domination has now produced a state of bitter and dangerous despondency throughout large parts of Eastern Europe. If the taste or even the hope for independence once dies out in the hearts of these peoples, then there will be no recovering it; then Moscow's victory will be complete. Eastern Europe will then be permanently lost to Europe proper and to the possibility of any normal participation in international life.

I can conceive of no escape from this dilemma that would not involve the early departure of Soviet troops from the satellite countries. Recent events have made it perfectly clear that it is the presence of these troops, coupled with the general military and political situation in Europe, which lies at the heart of the difficulty. Only when the troops are gone will there be possibilities for the evolution of these nations toward institutions and social systems most suited to their needs; and what these institutions and systems might then be is something about which I think we in the West can afford to be very relaxed. If socialism is what these people want and need, so be it; but let it by all means be their own choice.

Now it is plain that there can be no Soviet military withdrawal from Eastern Europe unless this entire area can in some way be removed as an object in the military rivalry of the Great Powers. But this at once involves the German problem. It involves the German problem not only because it implies the withdrawal of Soviet forces from Eastern Germany, but because so long as American and other Western forces remain in Western Germany it will be impossible for the Russians to view their problem in Eastern Europe otherwise than in direct relation to the over-all military equation between Russia and the West. Any solution of the problem of the satellite area is thus dependent on a solution of the German problem itself. This is one of the reasons why I am inclined to feel that the German question still stands at the center of world tensions; that no greater contribution can be made to world peace than the removal of the present deadlock over Germany, and that if, in fact, it is not removed, the chances for peace are very slender indeed.

This being the case, I think we cannot scrutinize too

closely or too frequently, in the light of the developing situation both in Europe and in the world at large, the position our governments have taken in the question of Germany in recent years.

We are all familiar with what that position has been. It is one that has insisted, and with very good reason, that the modalities of German unification, as a domestic program, must flow from the will of the German people, expressed in free elections. But it has gone farther than that. It has also insisted that no restrictions whatsoever must be placed in advance on the freedom of a future all-German government to determine its own international orientation and to incur military obligations to other states. Specifically, the Western governments have insisted that such an all-German government must be entirely free to continue to adhere to the NATO Pact, as the German Federal Republic does today; and it is taken everywhere as a foregone conclusion that an all-German government would do just that.

Now the question at once arises as to what would happen in such a contingency—in the contingency, that is, that a future united Germany should choose to adhere to NATO. What would happen then with the garrisons of the various Allied powers now stationed on German soil? The Western position says nothing specific about this. But the Soviet Union is, of course, not a member of NATO; and while British, French and American forces would presumably remain in Germany under the framework of the

NATO system, one must assume that those of the Soviet Union would be expected to depart. If this is so, then Moscow is really being asked to abandon—as part of an agreement on German unification—the military and political bastion in Central Europe which it won by its military effort from 1941 to 1945, and to do this without any compensatory withdrawal of American armed power from the heart of the Continent.

Now this, in my opinion, is something the Soviet Government is most unlikely to accept, if only for reasons of what it will regard as its own political security at home and abroad. It will be hard enough, even in the best of circumstances, for Moscow ever to extract itself from its present abnormal involvements in Eastern Europe without this having repercussions on its political system generally. It cannot, realistically, be asked—that is, it cannot be asked if agreement is wanted—to take this step in any manner that would seriously jeopardize its prestige. The Soviet leaders are not likely to be impressed with such paper assurance as the Western powers may undertake to give, to the effect that a unilateral withdrawal would not be exploited to Russia's disadvantage. The mere fact of Soviet withdrawal without any compensatory withdrawal on the Western side would create the general impression of a defeat for Soviet policy in Eastern and Central Europe generally.

The Soviet leaders will therefore see in these present Western proposals a demand for something in the nature of an unconditional capitulation of the Soviet interest in the German question generally; and it will surely occur to them that if they ever should be so weak as to have no choice but to quit Germany on these terms, it would scarcely take an agreement with the Western Powers to enable them to do so. So long, therefore, as it remains the Western position that the hands of a future all-German government must not be in any way tied in the matter of Germany's future military engagements, I see little hope for any removal of the division of Germany at all—nor, by the same token, of the removal of the division of Europe.

There are those in our Western camp, I know, who find in this state of affairs no great cause for alarm. A divided Germany seems, for the moment, to be less of a problem to them than was the united Germany of recent memory. They regard the continued presence of American forces in Germany as an indispensable pledge of American military interest in the Continent, and they tremble at the thought that this pledge should ever be absent. It is agreeable to them that America, by assuming this particular burden and bearing it indefinitely, should relieve Western Europe of the necessity of coming to grips itself with the German question.

This view is understandable in its way. There was a time, in the immediate postwar period, when it was largely justified. But there is danger in permitting it to harden into a permanent attitude. It expects too much, and for too long a time, of the United States, which is not a European power.

It does less than justice to the strength and the abilities of the Europeans themselves. It leaves unsolved the extremely precarious and unsound arrangements which now govern the status of Berlin—the least disturbance of which could easily produce a new world crisis. It takes no account of the present dangerous situation in the satellite area. It renders permanent what was meant to be temporary. It assigns half of Europe, by implication, to the Russians.

Let me stress particularly this question of Berlin. There is a stubborn tendency in our two countries to forget about the Berlin situation so long as it gives us no trouble and to assume that everything will somehow work out for the best. May I point out that the Western position in Berlin is by no means a sound or safe one; and it is being rendered daily more uncertain by the ominous tendency of the Soviet Government to thrust forward the East German regime as its spokesman in these matters. Moscow's purpose in this maneuver is obviously to divest itself of responsibility for the future development of the Berlin situation. It hopes by this means to place itself in a position where it can remain serenely aloof while the East German regime proceeds to make the Western position in the city an impossible one. This is a sure portent of trouble. The future of Berlin is vital to the future of Germany as a whole: the needs of its people and the extreme insecurity of the Western position there would alone constitute reasons why no one in the West should view the present division of Germany as a satisfactory permanent solution, even if no other factors were involved at all.

It would, of course, be wholly wrong to suggest that it is only the uncertainty of the Western position about the future of the garrisons in Germany that stands in the way of a settlement. I have no doubt that any acceptable arrangement for German unification would be an extremely difficult thing to achieve in any case. Many other obstacles would be bound to arise. It took ten years to negotiate a similar settlement for Austria. I can imagine that the negotiation of a German settlement might also take years, in the best of circumstances. But I think we are justified in assuming that it is this question of the indefinite retention of the American and other Western garrisons on German soil which lies at the heart of the difficulty; and until greater clarity is achieved about this point, there can be no proper beginning.

It will at once be held against what I have said that Moscow itself does not today want German unification on any terms. Perhaps so. Certainly in recent months there have been no signs of enthusiasm in Moscow for any settlement of this sort. But how much of this lack of enthusiasm is resignation in the face of the Western position, we do not know. Until we stop pushing the Kremlin against a closed door, we shall never learn whether it would be prepared to go through an open one. Today, our calculations about Moscow's reaction to proposals for a mutual withdrawal of forces

rest exclusively on speculation; for Moscow has been given
no reason to suppose that Western forces would under any
circumstances be withdrawn from the major portion of
Germany.

We must also bear in mind that things change from time
to time in Moscow, just as they do here in the West. If the
disposition to conclude a German settlement does not exist
today in Moscow, our positions should at least be such as to
give promise of agreement when and if this attitude changes.

Finally, the question is not just whether Moscow, as people say, "wants" German unification. It is a question of
whether Moscow could afford to stand in the way of it if
there were a real possibility for a general evacuation of
Europe. Gomulka not long ago promised the Polish people
that the day the Americans leave Germany, he will take up
with the Soviet Government the question of the departure
of the Soviet forces from Poland. And it is quite clear that
as Poland goes, in this respect, so goes the rest of the satellite
area. Khrushchev has not specifically demurred at Gomulka's position; on the contrary, he has, in fact, even
murmured things himself, from time to time, about a possible mutual withdrawal of forces, although he has inti-
mated that the price of a Soviet withdrawal might be somewhat higher than what Gomulka implied. In any case, the
interest of the satellite governments in a general evacuation
of Germany is perfectly clear. If, therefore, a more promising Western position would not assure agreement at this

time, it would at least serve to put a greater strain on Moscow's position, and to shift clearly and definitely to the Soviet side the onus of delaying a reasonable European settlement—an onus which in this case would have to be maintained against the feelings of many people in the satellite regimes as well as people elsewhere.

Are there, then, points at which the Western position could safely be improved? It is hard for an outsider to answer such a question in this rapidly moving time. Only governments are privy to all the relevant information. I can only say that there are two features of our present thinking which, in my opinion, might well undergo particular re-examination.

I wonder, in the first place, whether it is actually politic and realistic to insist that a future all-German government must be entirely free to determine Germany's military orientation and obligations, and that the victor powers of the recent war must not in any way prejudice that freedom by any agreement among themselves. This is outwardly a very appealing position. It gratifies the Western attachment to the principle of national self-expression. It is, for obvious reasons, a position no German politician can lightly oppose. We can hardly expect of the Germans that they should take the initiative in questioning it. But is it sound, and is it constructive?

A peace treaty has not yet been concluded. The powers of the victors have not yet formally lapsed in Germany. Might it not just be that the only politically feasible road to unification and independence for Germany should lie precisely through her acceptance of certain restraints on freedom to shape her future military position in Europe? And, if so, is it not just a bit quixotic to cling, in the name of the principle of German freedom and independence, to a position which implies the sacrifice of all freedom and all independence for many millions of Germans, namely the people of Eastern Germany, for an indefinite time to come? No useful purpose is going to be served by the quest for perfect solutions. The unlocking of the European tangle is not to be achieved except at some sort of a price. Is there not, in this insistence that the hands of a future German government must not be in any way tied, an evasion of the real responsibility the victor powers bear for resolving this present dangerous situation in Central Europe? This is, after all, a situation which they, not the Germans, created. Are they now to resign entirely to the Germans the responsibility for resolving it?

The second element of Western thinking about the German problem that might well stand further examination is the common assumption that the Western powers would be placed at a hopeless military disadvantage if there were to be any mutual withdrawal of forces from the heart of Europe.

It is, of course, impossible to discuss this question in specific terms unless one knows just what sort of withdrawal is envisaged—from where and to where, and by whom and when. Here, as is frequently forgotten, there are many possible combinations; and I am not at all sure that all of these have really been seriously explored by our planners.

But beyond this, I have the impression that our calculations in this respect continue to rest on certain questionable assumptions and habits of thought: on an overrating of the likelihood of a Soviet effort to invade Western Europe, on an exaggeration of the value of the satellite armies as possible instruments of a Soviet offensive policy, on a failure to take into account all the implications of the ballistic missile; and on a serious underestimation of the advantages to Western security to be derived from a Soviet military withdrawal from Central and Eastern Europe. I wonder how the military implications of a general withdrawal would appear if these distortions were removed.

People will ask: how do you envisage the future of Germany, if not as a full-fledged member of NATO? Is it neutrality you are recommending, or demilitarization, or a general European security pact?

These again are problems for the planners. The combinations are many; and they must be studied minutely, as alternatives. No outsider can judge which is best. I would only say that it seems to me far more desirable on principle to get the Soviet forces out of Central and Eastern Europe than to cultivate a new German army for the purpose of opposing them while they remain there. And as for a European security pact—well, I am no lover of security pacts and have, as a historian, never understood the great value other people still attach to them; but I cannot see that this sort of thing would necessarily invalidate the essential relationships of NATO. It cannot be stressed too often that NATO's real strength does not lie in the paper undertakings which underpin it; it lies—and will continue in any circumstances to lie—in the appreciation of the member nations for the identity of their real interests, as members of the Western spiritual and cultural community. If this appreciation is there, NATO will not be weaker, as a political reality, just because it may be supplemented or replaced by other arrangements so far as Germany is concerned.

I shall also be asked whether I am suggesting that Bonn should deal with the East German regime, as Mr. Khrushchev says it must if unification is ever to be arranged. This, I think, is very much Western Germany's own business. The German problem is not going to be solved, as things stand today, by Germans alone. Moscow, try as it may, cannot avoid its responsibility in this question; it is with Moscow that we Americans and British, in particular, at any rate, must deal.

The Kremlin would of course like to see the East German regime extort, as a price for unification, some sort of privileged and protected position for itself as a political faction within a future all-German state. This is obviously quite undiscussible. But it would seem to an outsider that people in Western Germany could afford to be very generous in defining the stages by which complete unification should be arrived at. Nothing could more foolish, on the West German side, than to let vindictiveness, intolerance or political passion block the road. The long period of Communist rule in Eastern Germany will have left strong marks on the structure of life there. There will certainly be a demand on the Communist side that not all these marks should be obliterated. Well, one can have one's own opinion as to whether they are positive or negative, whether they represent scars or achievements. But there is no reason why many of them should not be taken account of as facts, in any future settlement. Whether or not, for example, the industries of that region should remain socialized would seem to me, compared with what else is at stake, one of the least important of the problems in question.

My plea, then, is not that we delude ourselves that we can have a German settlement tomorrow; and it is not that we make frivolous and one-sided concessions to obtain one. My plea is only that we remember that we have a problem here, which must sooner or later be solved, and better sooner than later; and that we do our best to see that the positions we adopt with relation to it are at all times as hopeful and constructive as they can be made.

Now let me just add one last word on the general background of this German problem.

One of the arguments most frequently heard in opposition to the introduction of any greater flexibility into the Western position in Germany is that "you can't trust the Germans." It is therefore better, people say, that Germany should be held divided and in part dependent on the West, than that the Germans should once again be permitted independence of action as a nation. This is a judgment drawn, in the overwhelming majority of cases, from the unhappy experience of the past. Many of those who draw it are not acquainted with contemporary Germany.

I cannot share this opinion. Germany is in a state of great transition, and one can easily find, within its changing scene, anything one seeks. It is true that many of the older generation are not likely ever to recover entirely from the trauma of the past; they tend to be twisted people in one way or another, which does not necessarily mean that they are still Nazis. But I have seen, as an academic lecturer, whose own education took place partly in Germany, a bit of the younger Germany; and I am convinced that these young people, troubled, bewildered, unsupported at this time by any firm tradition from their own national past, will not fail to respond to any Western appeal that carries the ring of real vision, of conviction and of seriousness of purpose. The younger generation of Germans are more threatened today by the inroads of a pervasive cynical materialism than they are by any extreme nationalistic tendencies; and it is precisely here that we in the West have given them, I fear, little help or inspiration. To stake our future on this younger

Germany is admittedly to take a chance; but I can think of no greater risk than the trend toward nuclear war on which we are all now being carried.

If Germany cannot be accorded reasonable confidence in these coming years, then I would know of no promising solution to the entire problem of Europe. To assume that such confidence cannot be given is to cut ourselves off in advance from possibilities that may be vital to our very survival. If we are going to make so negative and so hopeless an assumption, let us be terribly, terribly sure that our judgment is drawn not from the memories and emotions of the past but from the soberest sort of attention to present realities.

CHAPTER IV.

The Military Problem

WHAT I have to speak about now is the military aspect of our conflict with Soviet power. It may seem strange, and scarcely fitting, that a civilian and common citizen, and a person not privy to governmental information, should venture to speak of it at all. But whoever thinks seriously about the problem of our relations with Russia cannot avoid doing his best to understand its military aspect, and making certain assumptions with regard to it.

There are few, I am sure, who will not agree that never in history have nations been faced with a danger greater than that which now confronts us in the form of the atomic weapons race. Except in instances where there was a possibility of complete genocide, past dangers have generally threatened only the existing generation. Today it is everything which is at stake—the kindliness of our natural environment to the human experience, the genetic composition of the race, the possibilities of health and life for future generations.

Not only is this danger terrible, but it is immediate.

Efforts toward composition of major political differences between the Russians and ourselves have been practically
abandoned. Belief in the inevitability of war—itself the
worst disservice to peace—has grown unchecked. We have
a world order marked by extreme instability. In the Middle
East alone we have a situation, any disturbance of which
could now easily involve us all in an all-out war. No one on
either side wishes this to occur; yet the complete uncertainty as to the adversary's intentions and the premium that
rests on the element of surprise in an atomic war could
easily cause people to take, under the pressure of fear or
misunderstanding, actions the effects of which would be
irreparable. It is against this terrible, immediate and almost
inconceivable danger that the risks of an effort to negotiate
a political settlement with Russia must today be measured.

To me it is a source of amazement that there are people
who still see the escape from this danger in the continued
multiplication by us of the destructiveness and speed of
delivery of the major atomic weapons. These people seem
unable to wean themselves from the belief that it is relative
changes in the power of these weapons that are going to
determine everything. They evidently believe that if the
Russians gain the slightest edge on us in the capacity to
wreak massive destruction at long range, they will immediately use it, regardless of our capacity for retaliation; whereas,
if we can only contrive to get a tiny bit ahead of the Russians,
we shall in some way have won; our salvation will be assured; the road will then be paved for a settlement on our

own terms. This cast of thought seems to have been much encouraged, in my own country at least, by the shock of the launching of the Russian earth satellites.

I scarcely need say that I see no grounds whatsoever in this approach. The hydrogen bomb, admittedly, has a certain sorry value to us today as a deterrent. When I say this, I probably do not mean exactly what many other people mean when they say it. I have never thought that the Soviet Government wanted a general world war at any time since 1945, or that it would have been inclined, for any rational political reason, to inaugurate such a war, even had the atomic weapon never been invented. I do not believe, in other words, that it was our possession of the atomic bomb which prevented the Russians from overrunning Europe in 1948 or at any other time. In this I have disagreed with some very important people.

But now that the capacity to inflict this fearful destruction *is* mutual, and now that this premium *has* been placed on the element of surprise, I am prepared to concede that the atomic deterrent has its value as a stabilizing factor until we can evolve some better means of protection. And so long as we are obliged to hold it as a deterrent, we must obviously see to it that it is in every way adequate to that purpose—in destructiveness, in speed of delivery, in security against a sudden preventative blow, and in the alertness of those who control its employment. I should certainly not wish to convey the impression that I have advocated anything like a neglect or slackening of our retaliatory capacity. But I can see no reason why we should indulge ourselves in the belief that the strategic atomic weapon can be anything more than a temporary and regrettable expedient, tiding us over a dangerous moment in world affairs. In particular, I see no reason to suppose that any sort of salvation or solution to our problems is to be found either in the increase of its speed of delivery and destructive power or in the cultivation of elaborate defenses against it.

So far as the effectiveness of the long-range atomic weapon as a deterrent is concerned, it is not the indefinite multiplication of its power which is important or relevant to our problem. It need only be terrible enough to make its use against us an irrational and self-defeating act on the part of any adversary. This it *has* been, in my opinion, for many years; and its effectiveness for this purpose is not going to be enhanced by its being made more terrible still.

And as for these various frantic schemes for defense against atomic attack, I can see no grounds whatsoever for confidence in them. I do not trust the calculations on which they are based. War has always been an uncertain exercise, in which the best-laid plans are frequently confounded. Today the variables and unknowns in these calculations are greater than ever before. I do not believe there is any human mind or group of human minds or any calculating machine anywhere in the world which can predict with accuracy what would happen if these weapons should begin to be used or which, by the same token, could devise realistic defenses against them.

But beyond this, what sort of a life is it to which these devotees of the weapons race would see us condemned? The technological realities of this competition are constantly changing from month to month and from year to year. Are we to flee like haunted creatures from one defensive device to another, each more costly and humiliating than the one before, cowering underground one day, breaking up our cities the next, attempting to surround ourselves with elaborate electronic shields on the third, concerned only to prolong the length of our lives while sacrificing all the values for which it might be worth while to live at all? If I thought that this was the best the future held for us, I should be tempted to join those who say, "Let us divest ourselves of this weapon altogether; let us stake our safety on God's grace and our own good consciences and on that measure of common sense and humanity which even our adversaries possess; but then let us at least walk like men, with our heads up, so long as we are permitted to walk at all." We must not forget that this is actually the situation in which many of the peoples of this world are obliged to live today; and while I would not wish to say that they are now more secure than we are, for the fact that they do not hold these weapons, I would submit that they are more secure than we would be if we were to resign ourselves entirely to the negative dynamics of the weapons race, as many would have us do.

The beginning of understanding rests, in this appalling problem, with the recognition that the weapon of mass destruction is a sterile and hopeless weapon which may for a time serve as an answer of sorts to itself and as an uncertain sort of shield against utter cataclysm, but which cannot in any way serve the purposes of a constructive and hopeful foreign policy. The true end of political action is, after all, to affect the deeper convictions of men; this the atomic bomb cannot do. The suicidal nature of this weapon renders it unsuitable both as a sanction of diplomacy and as the basis of an alliance. Such a weapon is simply not one with which one can usefully support political desiderata; nor is it one with which one readily springs to the defense of one's friends. There can be no coherent relations between such a weapon and the normal objects of national policy. A defense posture built around a weapon suicidal in its implications can serve in the long run only to paralyze national policy, to undermine alliances, and to drive everyone deeper and deeper into the hopeless exertions of the weapons race.

Now these thoughts are not mine alone. They are shared by many other people. They have been well expressed on other occasions. If I have seen fit to restate them here, it is to make clear my own position and to emphasize that their validity is in no way affected by the Soviet earth satellite, nor will it be affected if we launch a satellite ourselves.

But even among those who would go along with all that I have just said, there have recently been other tendencies of thought with which I also find myself in respectful but earnest disagreement. I have in mind here, in particular, the belief that the so-called tactical atomic weapon—the atomic weapon designed, that is, to be used at relatively short range against the armed forces of the adversary, rather than at long range and against his homeland—provides a suitable escape from the sterility of any military doctrine based on the long-range weapon of mass destruction.

Let me explain what I mean. A number of thoughtful people, recognizing the bankruptcy of the hydrogen bomb and the long-range missile as the bases for a defense policy, have pleaded for the simultaneous cultivation of other and more discriminate forms of military strength, and ones that could conceivably be used for some worth-while limited national objective, and without suicidal effect. Some have advocated a policy of what they call "graduated deterrents." Others have chosen to speak of the cultivation of the capacity for the waging of "limited war," by which they mean a war limited both in the scope of its objects and in the destructiveness of the weapons to be employed. In both instances what they have had in mind was to find an alternative to the hydrogen bomb as the basis for national defense.

One can, I think, have only sympathy and respect for this trend of thought. It certainly runs in the right direction. Force is, and always will be, an indispensable ingredient in human affairs; the alternative to a hopeless kind of force is never no-force-at-all. A first step away from the horrors of the atom must be the adequate development of agencies of force more flexible, more discriminate, and less suicidal in their effects. Had it been possible to develop such agencies in a form clearly distinguishable from the atomic weapon, this unquestionably would have provided the most natural path of escape from our present dilemma.

Unfortunately, this seems no longer to be an alternative, at least so far as the great nuclear powers are concerned. The so-called tactical atomic weapon is now being introduced into the armed forces of the United States and there is an intention, as I understand it, to introduce it into Great Britain. We must assume that the same thing is occurring in the Soviet Union. While many people in our respective governments have become convinced, I am sure, of the need for being able to fight limited as well as total wars, it is largely by the use of the tactical atomic weapon that they propose to fight them. It appears to be their hope that by cultivation of this tactical weapon we can place ourselves in a position to defend the NATO countries successfully without resorting to the long-range strategic one; that our adversaries can also be brought to refrain from employing the long-range one; that warfare can thus be restricted to whatever the tactical weapon implies; and that in this way the more apocalyptic effects of nuclear warfare may be avoided.

It is this thesis which I cannot accept. That it would prove possible, in the event of an atomic war, to arrive at some tacit and workable understanding with the adversary as to the degree of destructiveness of the weapons that would be used and the sort of target to which they would be directed, seems to me a very slender and wishful hope indeed.

But beyond this, let us bear in mind the probable ulterior effects—the effects, particularly, on the people in whose country such a war might be waged—of the use of tactical atomic weapons. There seems to be a cheerful assumption that these weapons are relatively harmless things, to be used solely against the armed forces of the enemy and without serious ulterior disadvantages. But surely this is not so! Even the tactical atomic weapon is destructive to a degree that sickens the imagination. If the experience of this century has taught us anything, it is that the long-term effects of modern war are by no means governed just by the formal outcome of the struggle in terms of victory or defeat. Modern war is not just an instrument of policy. It is an experience in itself. It does things to him who practices it, irrespective of whether he wins or loses. Can we really suppose that poor old Europe, so deeply and insidiously weakened by the ulterior effects of the two previous wars of this century, could stand another and even more horrible ordeal of this nature? Let us by all means think for once not just in the mathematics of destruction—not just in these grisly equations of probable military casualties—let us rather think of people as they are; of the limits of their strength, their hope, their capacity for suffering, their capacity for believing in the future. And let us ask ourselves in all seriousness how much worth saving is going to be saved if war now rages for the third time in a half-century over the face of Europe, and this time in a form vastly more destructive than anything ever known before.

Unfortunately, the danger is not even limited to the possible effects of the use of the tactical atomic weapon by our own English or American forces in time of war. There is a further contingent danger, and a very imminent one as things now stand; and this is that atomic weapons, strategic or tactical or both, may be placed in the arsenals of our continental allies as well.

I cannot overemphasize the fatefulness of such a step. I do not see how it could fail to produce a serious increase in the existing military tension in Europe. It would be bound to raise a grave problem for the Russians in respect of their own military dispositions and their relations with the other Warsaw Pact countries. It would inevitably bring about a further complication of the German and satellite problems. Moscow is not going to be inclined to entrust its satellites with full control over such weapons. If, therefore, the Western continental countries are to be armed with them, any Russian withdrawal from Central and Eastern Europe may become unthinkable once and for all, for reasons of sheer military prudence regardless of what the major Western Powers might be prepared to do.

In addition to this, it is perfectly obvious that the larger the number of hands into which the control over atomic weapons is placed, the smaller will be the possibility for their eventual exclusion from national arsenals by international agreement, and the more difficult it will be to preclude complications of all sorts. So long as only three great powers are involved, there is at least a chance that things can be kept under control. To place these weapons in the hands of a number of further countries is practically to assure that there can in future be no minor difficulty in Europe that does not at once develop into a major one.

I am aware that similar warnings against the introduction of the atomic weapon into the armaments of the continental countries have also recently been part of the stock-in-trade of Soviet diplomacy. I cannot know what the motives of the Soviet Government have been in taking this position. I certainly cannot say that they have all been ones we could respect. But I think we must beware of rejecting ideas just because they happen to coincide with ones put forward on the other side. Moscow says many harmful and foolish things; but it would be wrong to assume that its utterances never happen to accord with the dictates of sobriety and good sense. The Russians are not always wrong, any more than we are always right. Our task, in any case, is to make up our minds independently.

Is there, then, any reasonably hopeful alternative to the unpromising path along which we are now advancing? I must confess that I see only one. This is precisely the opposite of the attempt to incorporate the tactical atomic weapon into the defense of Western Europe. It is, again, the possibility of separating geographically the forces of the great nuclear powers, of excluding them as direct factors in the future development of political relationships on the Continent, and of inducing the continental peoples, by the same token, to accept a higher level of responsibility for the defense of the Continent than they have recently borne. This is still a possibility. Close as we are to it, we have not yet taken the fatal step. The continental countries have not yet prejudiced their usefulness for the solution of continental problems, as we have ours, by building their defense establishments around the atomic weapon. If they could be induced to refrain from doing this, and if there could be a general withdrawal of American, British and Russian armed power from the heart of the Continent, there would be at least a chance that Europe's fortunes might be worked out, and the competition between two political philosophies carried forward, in a manner disastrous neither to the respective peoples themselves nor to the cause of world peace. I would not know where else this chance is to be looked for.

I am aware that many people will greet this suggestion with skepticism. On the Continent, in particular, people have become so accustomed to the thought that their danger is a purely military one, and that their salvation can be assured only by others, that they rise in alarm at every suggestion that they should find the necessary powers of

resistance within themselves. There is a habitual underestimation among these peoples of the native resources of
Europe. The Western Europe of 1957 reminds me of the
man who has grown accustomed to swimming with water
wings and cannot realize that he is capable of swimming
without them.

It is plain that in the event of a mutual withdrawal of
forces, the continental NATO countries would still require,
in addition to the guarantees embodied in the NATO Pact,
some sort of continuing local arrangements for their own
defense. I am free to admit that for this purpose their existing conventional forces, based on the World War II pattern, would be generally inadequate. These conventional
forces are designed to meet only the least likely of the possible dangers: that of an outright Soviet military attack in
Europe, and then to meet it in the most unpromising manner, which is by attempting to hold it along some specific
territorial line. All of this is obviously futile. If this were
the problem, then of course foreign assistance would be
needed, although it is questionable whether it could ever
be enough.

But this is not the problem. We must get over this ob-
session that the Russians are yearning to attack and occupy
Western Europe, and that this is the principal danger. The
Soviet threat, as I have had occasion to say before, is a combined military and political threat, with the accent on the political. If the armed forces of the United States and Britain

were not present on the Continent, the problem of defense for the continental nations would be primarily one of the internal health and discipline of the respective national societies, and of the manner in which they were organized to prevent the conquest and subjugation of their national life by unscrupulous and foreign-inspired minorities in their midst. What they need is a strategic doctrine addressed to this reality. Under such a doctrine, armed forces would indeed be needed; but I would suggest that as a general rule these forces might better be paramilitary ones, of a territorial-militia type, somewhat on the Swiss example, rather than regular military units on the World War II pattern. Their function should be primarily internal rather than external. It is on the front of police realities, not on regular military battlefields, that the threat of Russian Communism must primarily be met. The training of such forces ought to be such as to prepare them not only to offer whatever overt resistance might be possible to a foreign invader but also to constitute the core of a civil resistance movement on any territory that might be overrun by the enemy; and every forethought should be exercised to facilitate their assumption and execution of this role in the case of necessity. For this reason they need not, and should not, be burdened with heavy equipment or elaborate supply requirements, and this means—and it is no small advantage—that they could be maintained at a fraction of the cost per unit of the present conventional establishments. I am inclined to wonder whether this concept could not well find application even as things are today, and in the absence of any Great Power withdrawal.

I would not wish to make a fetish of this or to suggest any sweeping uniform changes. The situations of no two NATO countries are alike. There are some that will continue to require, for various reasons, other kinds of armed forces as well. I mean merely to suggest that if there could be a more realistic concept of the problem and the evolution of a strategic doctrine more directly addressed to the Soviet threat as it really is and not as we have imagined it, the continental countries would not be as lacking in the resources or means for their own defense as is commonly assumed.

Let me reiterate that the primary purpose of the dispositions would be not the defense of the country at the frontier, though naturally one would aim to do whatever could be done in this respect, but rather its defense at every village crossroads. The purpose would be to place the country in a position where it could face the Kremlin and say to it: "Look here, you may be able to overrun us, if you are unwise enough to attempt it, but you will have a small profit from it; we are in a position to assure that not a single Communist or other person likely to perform your political business will be available to you for this purpose; you will find here no adequate nucleus of a puppet regime; on the contrary, you will be faced with the united and organized hostility of an entire nation; your stay among us will not be a happy one; we will make you pay bitterly for every day of it; and it will be without favorable long-term political prospects." I think I can give personal assurance that any country which is in a position to say this to Moscow, not in so many words, but in that language of military posture and political behavior which the Russian Communists understand best of all, will have little need of foreign garrisons to assure its immunity from Soviet attack.

CHAPTER V.

The Non-European World

EVER SINCE I had the temerity to mention the possibility of a political settlement in Europe, people have been saying to me: "Yes, but the Russians don't want a settlement." I have not denied this; on the other hand I cannot confirm it. I do not think we know what the Russians want; and I doubt that we are likely to find it out, so long as we persist in picturing it as something that exists in the abstract, independently of our own position and of what we might or might not be prepared to do in given contingencies.

But I think we might note that the Russian attitude in this question is going to be determined currently not just in the light of the situation in Europe but also in the light of developments in that great arc of territory that runs from China's southern frontier around through southern Asia and the Middle East to Suez and the north of Africa. Throughout this area things have generally been moving in recent years in a manner favorable to Soviet interests and unfavorable to our own. I can well understand that people in Moscow might wish to wait until they can see with greater clarity how far this process is going to carry, before they give serious consideration to a settlement in Europe. Why should the Kremlin commit itself in Europe so long as it feels that it has a good chance of turning our flank by the exploitation of our weakness in other areas?

Now there are significant differences between the situation in this southern band of states and the situation in Europe or in the area of Japan or Korea. In these places both we and the Russians have rights and formal relationships which cannot be unilaterally altered; and a future permanent status of these areas cannot very well be worked out except by negotiation and agreement between us. In the southern band of states, on the other hand, the formal status of the respective countries is not generally at stake, and there is little substance for negotiation between ourselves and Russia. Our problem in that part of the world is primarily one of the attitudes of the peoples who inhabit it. The things Moscow has been doing there—whether it be shipping arms or giving technical aid or making offers of trade or sending delegations around—however disturbing they may seem, are not things to which we can take formal objection. They are ones that are technically within the limits of international propriety. We do such things ourselves. We cannot ask the Russians to promise not to do them.

If the Western position has been deteriorating in many

parts of this area, this is because the peoples there have themselves been reacting in ways unfavorable to our interests. Moscow has been gratefully taking advantage of these reactions. But this is not a state of affairs which we can hope to improve by talking to people in Moscow. The Soviet leaders will see no reason—and I must confess that I can see none myself from their standpoint—why they should pass up golden opportunities to increase their own prestige and influence in an area which is largely uncommitted and of immense political importance. If the states of mind prevalent among the peoples of this area present Moscow with just such opportunities, this is a problem which we must tackle on the plane of our relationship with these peoples, not on the plane of our relationship with Moscow.

What are these attitudes which have played so powerfully into the Soviet's hands? They are difficult to describe because they assume so many forms. They vary from country to country—sometimes even from class to class. They differ with respect to their objects. The feelings directed to Englishmen, for example, are not always the same as those directed to Americans. Their origins lie in such diverse things as the emotional legacy of colonialism, resentments arising out of the color problem, jealousy over the material successes and outward affluence of certain Western countries, notably the United States, frustrations experienced by people who are for the first time bearing the responsibilities of power, an easy acceptance of Marxist clichés and symbols, and various prejudices and misapprehensions relating both to Russian society and to our own. Added to this are the impulses of a violent and sometimes irresponsible new nationalism—a nationalism which Moscow, having little to lose, has not hesitated to encourage, whereas the Western Powers, having more at stake, have been obliged to view it with concern and even to oppose it on a number of occasions. And, finally, because all political reactions are in a sense cumulative, there has been a widespread impression throughout these regions that the West, whatever its merits or deficiencies, was in any case on the decline, whereas the star of Moscow was rising; and this has not failed to impress that sizable portion of mankind which has more respect for power and success than it has for principle. In this bundle of impulses and reactions there is, in fact, something for everyone, something to appeal to every type of mind; and it is small wonder that it has all added up to a massive anti-Western complex, a complex in which a sneaking admiration for Western institutions and a desire to emulate them are mixed with a special, irritated sensitivity, an instinctive longing to see Western nations shaken and humbled, and a frequent inability to balance with any degree of realism the advantages of association with the West against those of association with Moscow. It is these states of mind, not what Mocow is doing to take advantage of them, which lie at the heart of our problem.

In this description of the origins of anti-Western feeling, I did not mention our own mistakes. This is not because we haven't made any—as we all know, there has been no lack of them—it is simply because I doubt that our mistakes have been among the root causes of this condition. I believe that this anti-Western animus has been primarily subjective in origin, and would have been there whatever we had done. On the other hand, there have been several tendencies in our recent behavior which certainly have not made things any better, and which I am afraid we have to face up to.

First of all, we have expected too much. Many of us seem to have believed that Russian influence could and should be excluded completely from this entire area. This attitude is surely unrealistic. It is perfectly natural that Russia, occupying the geographical position she does and being the great power she is, should have her place and her voice there too. By trying to persuade people that Russian influence has no place anywhere in this part of the world, we prepare in advance our own psychological defeats for the day when this turns out not to be in accord with political reality.

In addition to being unrealistic, this anxiety about Russian influence is often either unnecessary or exaggerated. Some of us seem to believe that no country can have anything to do with Moscow, even in the most normal ways, without at once losing its independence. Such a view exaggerates the sinisterness of Moscow's immediate purposes, which actually embrace a number of quite normal elements. It also involves an underestimation of the talent of Asian and African statesmen for seeing through the more dangerous long-term aspirations of international Communism and protecting their countries against them. Left to themselves, many of these statesmen would surprise us, I am sure, by their ability to take the measure of Moscow's motives and methods and to find resources of their own with which to protect the integrity of their national life.

I say *left to themselves* because it seems to me that we Americans, in particular, have not helped matters by sometimes showing ourselves overanxious about all this, by fussing over people, by acting as though it was we, rather than they, who had the most to lose if they went too far in their relations with Moscow. We have sometimes contrived to give them the impression that they would be reasonably safe, in fact, in playing close to the edge of danger, because if they got too close we could always be depended upon to come rushing in and rescue them with one sort of aid or another. We have even created a situation here and there where people believe they can exploit the threat of an unwise intimacy with Moscow as a means of bringing pressure to bear upon us. In this way, we have actually succeeded in dulling, to our own disadvantage, the sense of realism which these governments might normally have brought to their relations with the Soviet Union.

And we have, at the same time, done less than justice to our own position; for we have contrived to give an impression of weakness and jitteriness which has no justification in the realities of our situation. When suggestions are made to us that if aid of one sort or another is not forthcoming, people will, as the saying goes, "go Communist," surely there is only one answer: "Very well then, go. Our interests may suffer, but yours will suffer first." I sometimes wonder whether it is not true that only those are really worth helping who are determined to survive and to succeed whether one helps them or not.

Another mistake that we have made is to treat as though they were purely military problems dangers that were actually mainly psychological and political. Of all the countries of this great area, only certain ones in the Middle East have a common border with Russia; and even here I have not seen the evidence of a Soviet intention to launch any overt military aggression. There is, of course, what one might call a problem of ultimate defense in this area; and perhaps military pacts of one sort or another do have their usefulness in meeting it. But this is a problem which could become real only as part of a general war; to confuse it with the protection of this area from Communist penetration and domination in time of peace is simply to defeat our own purposes. To me, one of the most puzzling phenomena of this postwar era has been the unshakable conviction of so many people that the obvious answer to the threat of a growth of Communist influence is a military alliance or a military gesture.

The demands frequently made upon us by the independent countries in part of the world seem to me to run something like this: "We," they say, "are determined to have economic development and to have it at once. For us, this is an overriding aim, an absolute requirement; and we are not much concerned about the method by which it is achieved. You in the West owe it to us to let us have your assistance and to give it to us promptly, effectively, and without conditions; otherwise we will take it from the Russians, whose experience and methods we suspect anyway to be more relevant to our problems." In response to this approach, a great many people in my own country have come to take it for granted that there is some direct relationship between programs of economic aid on the one hand and political attitudes on the other—between the amount of money we are willing to devote to economic assistance in any given year and the amount of progress we may expect to make in overcoming these troublesome states of mind I have been talking about.

This thesis, as well as the reaction to it at home, seems to me to be questionable at every point. I find myself thrown off at the very start by this absolute value attached to rapid economic development. Why all the urgency? It can well be argued that the pace of change is no less important than its nature, and that great damage can be done by altering too rapidly the sociological and cultural structure of any society, even where these alterations may be desirable in themselves. In many instances one would also like to know how this economic progress is to be related to the staggering population growth with which it is associated. Finally, many of us in America have seen too much of the incidental effects of industrialization and urbanization to be convinced that these things are absolute answers to problems anywhere, or that they could be worth *any* sacrifice to obtain. For these reasons I cannot fully share the basic enthusiasm on which this whole thesis is founded.

I must also reject the suggestion that our generation in the West has some sort of a cosmic guilt or obligation vis-à-vis the underdeveloped parts of the world. The fact that certain portions of the globe were developed sooner than others is one for which I, as an American of this day, cannot accept the faintest moral responsibility; nor do I see that it was particularly the fault of my American ancestors. I cannot even see that the phenomenon of colonialism was one which could be regarded as having given rise to any such state of obligation. The establishment of the colonial relationship did not represent a moral action on somebody's part; it represented a natural and inevitable response to certain demands and stimuli of the age. It was simply a stage of history. It generally took place with the agreement and connivance of people at the colonial end as well as in the mother country. Nor were the benefits derived from this relationship in any way one-sided. The Marxists claim, of course, that colonialism invariably represented a massive and cruel exploitation of the colonial peoples. I am sure that honest study would reveal this thesis to be quite fallacious. Advantages, injuries and sacrifices were incurred on both sides. Today these things are largely bygones. We will do no good by scratching around to discover whose descendants owe the most to the descendants of the other. If we are to help each other in this world, we must start with a clean slate.

I can well understand that there are instances in which it will be desirable for us from time to time to support schemes of economic development which are soundly conceived and which give promise, over the long run, of yielding greater stability and a new hopefulness for the countries concerned. I trust that we will not let such demands go unanswered when they arise. There is no fonder hope in the American breast, my own included, than that the experience we have had in developing a continent will prove relevant and helpful to others. Every American would like to see us take a useful part in solving problems of economic development elsewhere in the world. But action of this sort can be useful only if it proceeds on a sound psychological basis. If there is a general impression in the recipient countries that this aid represents the paying of some sort of a debt from us to them, then the extension of it can only sow confusion. The same is true if it is going to be interpreted as a sign of weakness on our part or of a fear that others might go over to the Communists, or if it is going to be widely attacked in the recipient countries as evidence of what the Communists have taught people to refer to as "imperialism," by which they seem to mean some sort of intricate and concealed foreign domination, the exact workings of which are never very clearly explained.

Unless such reactions can be ruled out, programs of economic aid are apt to do more harm than good, psychologically; and it ought properly to be the obligation of the recipient governments and not of ourselves to see that these misinterpretations do not occur. To those who come to us with requests for aid one would like to say: "You tell us first how you propose to assure that if we give you this aid it will not be interpreted among your people as a sign of weakness or fear on our part, or of a desire to dominate you."

These are not the only psychological dangers of foreign aid. There is the basic fact that any form of benevolence, if prolonged for any length of time (even in personal life this is true), comes to be taken for granted as a right and its withdrawal resented as an injury. There is the fact that any program of economic development represents a change in the terms of competition within a country and brings injury to some parties while it benefits the others. It is hard to give aid to any other country economically without its having an effect on internal political realities there—without its redounding to the benefit of one political party and the disadvantage of another.

All these considerations incline me to feel that, desirable as programs of foreign aid may sometimes be from the long-term standpoint, their immediate psychological effects are apt to be at best mixed and uncertain. For this reason, foreign aid, as a general practice, cannot be regarded as a very promising device for combating, over the short term, the psychological handicaps under which Western statesmanship now rests in Asia and Africa.

Finally, I do not think for a moment that the Soviet Union really presents the alternative people seem to think it represents to a decent relationship with the West. Moscow has its contribution to make to what should be a common task of all the highly industrialized countries; and there is no reason why this contribution should not be welcomed wherever it can be really helpful. But Moscow is not exactly the bottomless horn of plenty it is often held to be; and it is rather a pity that it has never been required to respond all at once to the many expectations directed to it. We ourselves should be the last, one would think, to wish to spare it this test. The results might be both healthy and instructive.

What, then, is there to be done about these feelings of people in Asia and Africa? Very little, I am afraid, over the short term, except to relax, to keep our composure, to refuse to be frightened by the Communism alternative, to refrain from doing the things that make matters worse, and to let things come to rest, as in the end they must, on the sense of self-interest of the peoples concerned. The only place where we have an urgent and dangerous problem today, which admittedly demands something more than the long-term approach, is the Middle East.

Here, it seems to me, the essence of Western policy must lie in preventing the unsettled state of this area from leading to world war. It would be wholly unrealistic, I think, to suppose that the future development of relationships here can occur everywhere without violence. If we are going to go on bestowing the quality of absolute sovereignty on new political entities at the rate of approximately one a year, as we have been doing for the past fifty years, without much regard to the degree of political maturity and experience which they bring to the exercise of this responsibility, then I think we must expect that armed conflict on a local scale is going to continue to be a frequent feature of the political scene in any area of the world where these raw sovereignties predominate. The Middle East is such an area. On top of this general situation we have, in this instance, a special and most tragic source of instability in the failure of the Arab world to accept the establishment of the State of Israel.

Now it has long been a common platitude of international discourse, despite much evidence to the contrary, that peace is indivisible. I should certainly hope that this is not true of the Middle East; for, if it were, there would be little chance of avoiding a world war. Our concern should surely be not to seek the answer to all Middle

Eastern problems by undertaking to involve in their solution the armed forces of the Great Powers, but precisely to find ways by which this can be avoided. Any entry of Russian or American forces into the Middle East, whether under United Nations auspices or not, will produce reactions elsewhere which it would be better not to arouse.

Let us, of course, do everything we can to discourage hostilities in that part of the world. To this end let us seek to reconcile and unify where we can, not to divide. But let us at the same time be careful not to place ourselves in a position where such hostilities as cannot be avoided would inevitably have to involve us all. Short of the entry of Soviet troops into this area, there is nothing that could happen there that would be worth the cost of a world war. With anything else, we could eventually cope.

It will be pointed out that the security of the Western world not only can be, but is being, jeopardized by the fact that local regimes strongly hostile to the Western Powers and vulnerable to Soviet influence control resources and facilities that are important, if not vital, to our security. This is, of course, the situation that prevails today in Egypt and Syria. It could prevail elsewhere tomorrow.

I can see only one answer to this situation which would not enhance the chances of a world war, and that is that we should act with determination to reduce our dependence on the resources and facilities in question. This can be done in a number of ways, and each of them should probably have some place in Western policy. It can be done by cultivating alternatives to the use of these raw-material sources or facilities; it can be done by stock-piling; it can be done, in certain instances, by placing minor limitations on consumption at home. These possibilities were extensively discussed, and to some extent practiced, at the time of the Suez crisis. I can see no reason why they should be ignored today. The purpose of such measures would not be to free ourselves entirely from the use of Middle Eastern oil or the Suez Canal. Nothing so drastic would be necessary. The purpose would be to give us greater flexibility in our dealings with the countries concerned and to restore something of that basic bargaining power which was so woefully and conspicuously lacking at the time of Suez.

The fact is that until we learn to live without these people we shall find it hard to learn to live with them. I was never able to understand why we were in such a hurry, a year ago, to be permitted to repair the Suez Canal and the Syrian pipeline at our own expense—and this at a time when we were doing much better than people thought we should have done in learning to get along without them. We were on the right road; this road is still open to us today. I am sure that we would not have to go very far in the development of alternatives to an unhealthy reliance on the oil and such facilities of the Middle East before we would see in the reactions of the governments concerned signs of a new and more realistic sense of self-interest.

I have no illusion that this development of alternatives will be easy for us to accomplish. It involves all those things that seem to be most difficult for our governments in times other than those of the most pressing danger. It involves intimate Anglo-American collaboration, not just sporadically in occasional conferences but in day-to-day operations. It involves the co-ordination of the operations of great private concerns with those of government. It may well even involve measures of domestic self-denial—a thing which for some reason our peoples seem to regard as unthinkable except in moments of greatest military extremity.

I am sorry that the demand is such a harsh one. But it represents actually only a small part of that obligation of greater national discipline that we are now going to have to accept generally if we are to have any hope of making headway in our competition with Russia.

People talk a great deal these days about the need for a new sense of urgency, and they are right to do so. I believe that this competition can be carried forward successfully without the disasters of another war. But I do not believe for a moment that this is a race which is to be run without dust and heat. It is the essence of our present situation that the dust and the heat must be incurred now, in a period of nominal peace and outward normality; they will do us no good if we wait, this time, till the last moment. If such things as a tighter economic discipline and a curb on certain forms of consumption in our countries are the price of the restoration of a sound Western position in the competition with Soviet power, I think it a cheap one compared with what else is at stake.

Measures along the lines I have suggested here will not bring us success everywhere. The deterioration has been in some respects greater than we like to admit. There will be instances where it will be best for us to cut our losses; and in this case, I see no reason why the burden should not be fairly shared throughout the Atlantic Pact community. But what is important is that the dignity of the Western position in Asia and Africa should be restored and that the situation should be stabilized at some point. With the proper investment of realism and determination, such a point can, I am sure, be established. The diplomatic assets of Western Europe and North America are not yet so small that they would not suffice, under co-ordinated and purposeful direction, to accomplish this purpose. Once people in Moscow see that such a point does exist, and that what lies to our side of it is enough to assure our security and to leave us the ability to carry on indefinitely as a major factor in world affairs—once they see, in other words, that we are not really to be outflanked in the Asian and African theaters or any other—then I am sure they will not be long in appreciating the advantages to themselves of a fair settlement of political differences in the key areas of Europe and of Northeast Asia.

CHAPTER VI.

Strengthening NATO— to What End?

WHEN THESE talks were first conceived some months ago, it was my thought to speak, on this occasion, not of the issues confronting our respective governments at this moment, but of the impact which you in England and we in America have on each other as peoples.* I wanted to talk about the similarity of our problems, domestic and foreign; about the foolishness of regarding each other's concerns as something external to ourselves; and about the much greater foolishness of supposing that either of us might stand to gain anything from the reverses and misfortunes of the other. In thinking to talk of these things I had in mind, of course, the unfortunate psychological effects of Suez and other sources of misunderstanding and difference between us.

Today, after four months in England, I find it no longer necessary to speak of these things. A new combination of

* See Chapter VII, which was not delivered in this lecture series.

circumstances and preoccupations has come into being which has made us all feel, I think, that Suez, as an episode, is now very far away indeed.

The heads of our respective governments are at this moment convening in Paris to reaffirm the purposes of the North Atlantic alliance and to see what can be done to make it a stronger instrument for resisting aggression, and everyone senses the extraordinary importance that attaches to their deliberations. It will not be useful now for an outsider to speak of the specific questions they will have before them.

But the occasion is, perhaps, not an unsuitable one for reflecting on the ultimate goal that underlies whatever we do within the framework of NATO. What is it specifically that this organization, and the other Western efforts to meet the Soviet challenge (because NATO is only one of them), are supposed to achieve? To what end are they tending?

To read recent statements of the Soviet leaders, one would think that the only purpose behind the entire NATO operation was the preparation and eventual unleashing of a preventive war. For years it has been standard propaganda practice in Moscow never to refer to this alliance except as the "aggressive NATO pact."

Now, there may be a few people here and there in the Western countries who would welcome the idea of another war, as a means of dealing with world Communism, and who would think it our business to start it. I cannot recall ever meeting one. Their number, in any case, would scarcely include a single person whose opinion carries weight. The Soviet leaders could make no more useful contribution to the cause of peace, and none that would cost them less, than the abandonment of this absurd and dangerous suggestion. There may be much bewilderment and some real confusion of thought behind the operations of NATO; there may have been statements, here and there, that were subject to misinterpretation. But there is certainly no desire in any responsible Western quarter for another world war, or any intention to unleash one if it can possibly be avoided. If people in Moscow do not already know this, they have ample means for finding it out.

A much more understandable concept of NATO's purpose, though also unsound and incorrect, is that entertained by those who have permitted themselves to view another war as inevitable, either because they expect that the Russians will themselves start it, or because they believe that governments will be carried into it, whether they so desire or not, by the dynamics of political conflict and the weapons race. And, having resigned themselves to the inevitability of war, these people tend to say: let us put aside all other considerations; let us arm to the teeth and with greatest urgency; let us see whether we cannot make our military dispositions such that, when the moment does come, we may at least survive. And it is to NATO that these people naturally look, as one of the major instruments of survival.

Of this view, which ignores the destructiveness of modern weapons and exaggerates the significance of relative changes in military capabilities in this age of nuclear plenty, I have said what I had to say in previous talks. Suffice it to observe here that if the end of our present course were plainly an all-out nuclear war, then any other course would be better.

A third concept of NATO's purpose might be called the cultivation of military strength as a background for an eventual political settlement on our own terms, and without the necessity of compromise. Those who entertain this concept are generally people who have a strong sense of moral righteousness about Western purposes. They believe that once it has been demonstrated to Moscow that successful aggression in Western Europe is not militarily feasible, the Soviet leaders will either appreciate the merit of Western *desiderata* or understand the futility of opposing them, and will retract generally from their present international posture. The West will thus be spared the necessity of compromising its aspirations or of negotiating about matters which, as these people see it, are too important in principle to be the subject of negotiation. I hope I do not do too much injustice to the views of these people by this sketchy summary.

This is, from the standpoint of the number and influence of those who entertain it, a much more serious concept than the other I have mentioned. So far as I can see, it has recently had currency in wide and influential circles of Western opinion.

But this view, too, has weaknesses, the recognition of which is vital to the present discussion of NATO policy. It seems to rest, in the first place, on an assumption that Soviet unwillingness to accept Western proposals, particularly the proposals for Europe's future and for general disarmament, arises from the fact that the NATO forces are not as strong as they might be.

I see little evidence for this reasoning. The Soviet reluctance to withdraw from Eastern Germany and to give full freedom to the Eastern European peoples is based partly on political considerations that would not be in any way affected by a stronger NATO, and partly on the existence of precisely that Anglo-American military position on the continent which it is now proposed that we should reinforce.

And it is difficult to believe that a stronger NATO, particularly one that would include missile launching sites on the Continent or the presence of atomic weapons in the arsenals of the continental countries, would increase the inclination of the Soviet Government to accept recent Western disarmament proposals. It might conceivably have this effect if the West were able to offer to withdraw these dispositions as part of an eventual bargain. But elaborate military arrangements of this nature, once put in hand, have consequences. They produce counter measures on the other side. People come to depend on them as essential elements of their security. In the end it becomes difficult to consider their withdrawal or to make them the subject of negotiation. And besides, it is not easy to see what *quid pro quo* Moscow could be expected to extend in the specific matter of atomic weapons in Europe beyond the offer it has already made to refrain from stationing nuclear weapons in Eastern Germany, Poland and Czechoslovakia. If this offer is not acceptable today, is there reason to suppose it would be more acceptable tomorrow?

I suspect that this view of NATO's purpose, which sees in the alliance a device for avoiding political compromise rather than for facilitating it, rests on these same illusions of relative advantage in the weapons race to which I had occasion to refer in an earlier talk. People think, that is, that if our weapons could only be made a bit stronger than those on the other side, our negotiating position would be just that much better. But if the relative size of the capacity for destruction is becoming increasingly questionable as a military advantage, is it probable that it will have any greater political significance?

How, then, should NATO's purpose be conceived?

When I ask myself this question, my mind goes back to the days in 1948 when the NATO pact was in process of negotiation. I was myself for a time chairman of the working-level subcommittee in which the language of the terms of the pact was thrashed out. Those were hopeful and exciting days. The European Recovery Program, enthusiastically supported on both sides of the water, was then just yielding its first constructive results. There were, of course, even at that time, problems and complications. Europe's economic difficulties were still bitter. The attitude of the Soviet Government was not one whit less disturbing than it is today; on the contrary, Stalin was very much alive, and Moscow was just then preparing the political offensive against Western Europe which later culminated in the Berlin blockade. And if Russia did not yet have atomic weapons, there was no reason to suppose she would not have them, sooner or later.

And yet we were not downhearted, and our eyes were not riveted, as I recall it, on the military balance in Europe, which was actually much less favorable at that time than it is today. I cannot speak here for my friends and colleagues on that subcommittee, but I certainly had no idea at that time that the military instrument we were creating was to be the major vehicle of Western policy in the coming years. It seemed to me that we were setting up a military shield, required less by any imminent actual danger than by the need for a general stabilization of the situation in Europe and for reassurance of the Western European peoples in the light of Soviet military superiority and of their own somewhat traditional and subjective anxieties about land invasion. And behind this shield, I supposed, we would go ahead confidently to meet the Communist danger in its most threatening form—as an internal problem, that is, of Western society; to be combated by reviving economic activity, by restoring the self-confidence of the European peoples, and by helping them to find positive goals for the future.

The Marshall Plan, some of us thought, would be only the beginning: it would lay the foundation for a new sense of purpose in Western society—a sense of purpose needed not just for our protection against an outward threat but to enable us to meet a debt to our own civilization—to become what we ought to be in the light of our traditions and advantages—to accomplish what we would have owed it to ourselves to accomplish, even had such a thing as international Communism never existed. In this vision we saw a new ordering of international relations generally in the Atlantic and European areas, designed to provide an alternative for peoples who stood at the crossroads in a Europe where the old values had lost their relevance; and it was our hope that this alternative could be made so patently worthy and inspiring in itself, and so wholly without menace to anyone anywhere, that peoples could safely repair to it without raising military issues, without raising questions of great power prestige.

This was the concept around which, outstandingly, the Marshall Plan was built. Only by this means, it seemed to us, could one loosen the great political cramp by which postwar Europe was already beginning to be seized. Only by this means was there any hope that the confused termination of one war could be prevented from growing imperceptibly into the origins of another, and this time one in which all European values would finally perish.

In all of this NATO had, as a military alliance, its part to play; but I think every one of us hoped that its purely military role would decline in importance as the curse of bipolarity fell from the Continent, as negotiations took place, as armies were withdrawn, as the contest of ideologies took other forms. The central agency in this concept was not NATO but the European Recovery Program; and none of us dreamed at that time that the constructive impulses of this enterprise, which looked to everyone so hopeful in those days, would be overtaken and swallowed up in the space of a mere two or three years by programs of military assistance based on a wholly different concept of the Soviet threat and of Europe's needs.

I am not attempting to assign blame for this transformation that has come over the general idea of what we were attempting to accomplish as we approached international Communism. I do not mean to belittle the real changes introduced into our situation by the Soviet acquisition of the nuclear capability and by the appalling advances achieved in the frightfulness of atomic weapons. I do not wish to suggest that the problems faced by our statesmen in this intervening period have been light ones or that the alternatives to this deterioration would have been easy ones to discover and to adopt. Least of all do I mean to absolve the Communists from their share of responsibility for this militarization of thinking about what should never have been regarded at all as a military conflict. Few decisions have ever caused more psychological damage or produced more dangerous confusion than that which started the Korean war in 1950. And this was only one instance of the damage done from the Moscow side.

But I should like to raise today the question whether anything has really happened to invalidate this original concept on which both Marshall Plan and NATO were founded, whether the positive goals of Western policy have really receded so far from the range of practical possibility as to be considered eclipsed by the military danger, whether we would not, in fact, be safer and better off today if we could put our military fixations aside and stake at least a part of our safety on the earnestness of our effort to do the constructive things, the things for which the conditions of our age cry out and for which the stage of our technological progress has fitted us.

Surely everyone, our adversary no less than ourselves, is tired of this blind and sterile competition in the ability to wreak indiscriminate destruction. The danger with which it confronts us is a common danger. The Russians breathe the same atmosphere as we do, they die in the same ways. Problematical as I believe the psychology of the Soviet leaders to be, I cannot warn too strongly against the quick assumption that there is no kernel of sincerity in all these messages with which they have been bombarding the Western chancelleries in recent weeks. Their idea of peace is, of course, not the same as ours. There will be many things we shall have to discuss with them about the meaning of this term before we can agree on very much else. But I see no reason for believing that there are not, even in Moscow's interpretation of this ambiguous word, elements more helpful to us all than the implications of the weapons race in which we are now caught up. And I refuse to believe that there is no way in which we could combine a search for these elements with the pursuit of a reasonable degree of military security in a world where absolute security has become an outmoded and dangerous dream.

Now let me just mention—because this seems to be the heart of the difficulty—what such a concept would *not* mean. It would not imply, first of all, that military strength would not continue to be cultivated on our side until we have better alternatives. The Soviet radio claims that to recognize, as I have done in these talks, that Russia is not yearning to launch an attack on Western Europe means, and I quote their words: "To give up the whole of NATO, the United States bases, and the enormous military expenditure"; in short, the entire Western military structure. What utter nonsense! As though we did not know that any sudden and unilateral Western disarmament would create new political situations and new invitations to aggression where none existed before. Armaments are important not just for what could be done with them in time of war, but for the psychological shadows they cast in time of peace. No one here has forgotten, I trust, the basic hostility borne us by world Communism, the never-ending abuse of our institutions, the shameless distortion of our realities before world opinion, the cynical principles of political struggle, and the sharp, ruthless political tactics that have marked the Russian Communist movement since the moment of its inception. We know what we are up against. Let no one suppose that a recognition of the horrors of nuclear war is going to lead logically to a political and military capitulation on the Western side, any more than it will on the other.

What flows from what I have said is not that one should give up unilaterally the nuclear deterrent, or even that one should desist from the effort to strengthen the NATO forces in Europe. What flows from what I have said is only that war must not be taken as inevitable; that one must not be carried away by the search for absolute security; that certain risks must be assumed in order that greater ones may be avoided; and that NATO must not be strengthened in such a way as to prejudice the chances for an eventual reduction, by peaceful negotiation, of the danger of an all-out war.

Under the concept I have outlined, the military dispositions of NATO would not be an end in themselves but only the means to an end. And this end would not be the achievement of any total solution in the sense of a sudden removal of the political rivalry between the Communist system and our own. It would be the piecemeal removal, by negotiation and compromise, of the major sources of the military danger, particularly the abnormal situation now prevailing in Central and Eastern Europe, and the gradual achievement of a state of affairs in which the political competition could take its course without the constant threat of a general war. There is no use looking any further than this. Our first concern must be to achieve what is, or might be, immediately possible. After that, we shall see.

And not only can the strengthening of NATO *not* be a substitute for negotiation, but NATO cannot itself provide either the source of authority or the channel for the negotiating process. The governmental structures of the individual NATO members are already of such ponderous and frightening complexity in themselves that it sometimes seems to me questionable whether they would be capable of providing the imagination, the privacy of deliberation, the speed of decision, and the constancy of style necessary to the pursuit of any delicate diplomatic undertaking, even if they were not encumbered with their obligations to allies. What will the situation be if we multiply the ponderousness by a factor of fifteen? A negotiating position into which there is assiduously inserted every last inhibition of every one of fifteen governments will never be a position sufficiently bold and generous to serve as a proper basis for composing issues as complex and stubborn as those that must now be cleared away between Russia and the West. This talk will have to be tackled first by individual governments, within the limits of their competence and with reference to those objects of controversy which lie within their control. The main outlines of settlement will then have to find, at the proper time and in the proper way, the understanding and acquiescence of those whose responsibilities are less directly involved.

It is also idle to suppose that the strengthening of NATO could alone provide the necessary climate and background for negotiation. It cannot be too often reiterated that our contest with Soviet power is of so pervasive and subtle a nature that our purpose cannot be served by any single agency of policy, such as the military one. It is the sum total of our performance that counts; our effort must embrace all facets of our national behavior. Moscow fights with all the political and psychological means at its command; and it will know how to take advantage, as indeed it already has in many ways, of any one-sided concentration of effort on our part. This is why we cannot afford to put all our eggs in the military basket and neglect the positive purposes—the things which we ought to be doing, and would be doing, if the military threat were not upon us at all. The fortunes of the cold war will begin to turn in our direction as and when we learn to apply ourselves resolutely to many things that have, superficially viewed, nothing whatsoever to do with the cold war at all.

Let us, then, while keeping our guard up and while never ceasing to explore the possibilities for progress by negotiation, not neglect those undertakings that are necessary for the spiritual and economic advancement of Western society. There is so much to be done. Our friends on the Continent have recently made exciting progress, despite all military danger, in welding the economic and technological efforts of the Western European peoples into a single competitive yet collaborative whole, and in moderating the sharp edges of that absolute sovereignty which is one of the anachronisms of our time. All power to them; and all admiration for having had the steadfastness to get on with these things at the time when the sputnik was whirling overhead. Surely there is room for something of the same courage and vision in the ordering of the relationships between England, Canada and the United States: for the overcoming of the pound-dollar division and the establishment of common policies in those areas where our concerns and responsibilities are common. This, too, was envisaged in the original Marshall Plan concept; but it was one of the things that got lost somewhere in the military shuffle. Can it not today be recovered? There is nothing in all this that need worry our continental allies. It changes nothing in our military commitments and arrangements. Is it not perfectly clear that NATO will never be stronger than the degree of intimacy and collaboration that prevails within its English-speaking component?

This is only an example of the things that await doing on the international level, but beyond this there is the whole great area of domestic affairs. Let us not forget this, precisely in the present connection. Many of us dislike to think of domestic problems as battlefields on which, again, our contest with Soviet power is transpiring; but that is exactly what they are. In a thousand ways, the tone and spirit that characterize our internal life impinge themselves on our external fortunes.

Our diplomacy can never be stronger than the impression we contrive to create on others, not just by virtue of what we *do* but rather—and even more importantly—by what we *are*. What greater error could there conceivably be than the belief that weapons, however terrible, could ever protect selfishness, timidity, shortsightedness and lassitude from the penalty that awaits them, over the long run, in the general competition of international life? What greater error than to suppose that such things as courage and vigor and confidence cannot assert themselves in world affairs without the aid of the hydrogen bomb?

Russia confronts us not just with a foreign policy or a military policy but with an integrated philosophy of action, internal and external. We can respond effectively in no other way.

Let us not look, therefore, to the council tables of NATO to provide the basic strength on which the security of the Western world must rest. The statesmen there can work only with what they have. Of this, the armies and weapons are only the smaller part. The greater part lies still in what we of this generation are—first of all to ourselves, secondarily to others. If it is really a new wind that needs to blow through our lives, to enable us to meet successfully the scorn and hostility brought to us by world Communism, then let us open our windows to it and let us brace ourselves to the buffeting we must expect.

In the conclusion of the X-article, to which I referred at the outset of these talks, I cited a passage from the American writer Thoreau. Today, under the shadow of the hydrogen bomb and of all the materialism and faint-heartedness of our time, I am going to recall this passage to mind once more. It is, unfortunately, even more relevant today than it was ten years ago.

"There is no ill," Thoreau wrote, "which may not be dissipated, like the dark, if you let in a stronger light upon it. . . . If the light we use is but a paltry and narrow taper, most objects will cast a shadow wider than themselves."

CHAPTER VII.

Anglo-American Relations

IN ONE OF THE earlier lectures, I spoke of the persistent tendency of the Soviet leaders to pursue their objectives by attempting to sow disunity in the adversary's camp rather than by serious negotiation and compromise.

There is no instance where this desire has been more intense and of longer standing than in the case of Anglo-American relations. From the very day of the Revolution, for years on end—in Lenin's time and in Stalin's—the prospect of a conflict between England and America was consistently hailed by the Soviet leadership as the greatest single factor favoring, and in fact assuring, the eventual success of the world Communist revolution. To no other possibility have Soviet hopes ever been so intently riveted.

Behind this fixation there lay a wholly sound political instinct. A certain minimum of Anglo-American solidarity —and this means in effect Anglo-*Canadian*-American solidarity—is absolutely essential to the capacity of the old world to stand up in the face of the pressures being brought to bear against it in our age. I may be right or I may be

wrong in the views on specific matters of policy which I
have put forward here; but of this you may be certain: the
day that Englishmen and Americans come to regard their
mutual differences as more important than the need for a
common front in the face of Communist power in Russia,
there will no longer be any future for any nation in the
Western world. Conversely, so long as the minimum of
Anglo-American solidarity is preserved—so long as the
English-speaking nations continue to manifest in their own
mutual relations the genius for tolerance and accommodation that lies at the heart of their domestic life—the Communist victory will never be complete and the ideals of
Soviet Communism will never remain without serious
challenge.

This Anglo-American solidarity has received, during the
past year or two, a very severe buffeting—to Moscow's intense delight.

It is for this reason that I feel unable to end a series of
talks on the Russian problem without a few words on the
thorny and much discussed subject of our mutual relations.

This is, of course, not the easiest of times to be an American in England or to talk about being one. Polite as everyone usually is, no sensitive person from my country can be
wholly unaware here of the negative feelings that do exist
about us.

To react to these sentiments is no simple matter. We
Americans cannot entirely play the innocent and the mis-

understood. We have our deficiencies. We often irritate and offend people. We are much less conscious than others normally are of the difference between the advantages we have and the conditions under which others have been obliged to live in recent years. Americans are generally interested in their own country and pleased about its progress; and they have a tendency to blabber on about these things, assuming that others will be equally pleased and interested, and quite unaware of the fact that they are raising painful comparisons and touching people on sensitive spots. What is really good will and perhaps a certain effort to compensate for the sense of insecurity one finds in a foreign land thus comes to appear as arrogance and ostentation. This is all very reprehensible. Nothing is more maddening than an unfeeling innocence. It represents, no doubt, a national fault; and we must endeavor to overcome it.

On the other hand, we are obliged to recognize that in the intensity of the negative reactions of others to Americans and to things American there is a strong component that is entirely subjective in origin for which we cannot feel ourselves in any way to blame. Envy is obviously not entirely lacking here; and we are not comforted by the fact that the image of what our life is like—the image for which people envy us—usually bears little relation to reality. We know that our own lives are not as easy as they look to others. We know that many of our people work very hard for what they get—harder, in some instances, than do people on the other side of the water. I can recall, for example, the difficulty I once had in explaining to people in my village why it was desirable that we should ship coal to England under the Marshall Plan when our coal miners were working longer hours than were the men in the British mines. We feel, in other words, that we should be entitled to some credit for hard work and for a considerable practicality and inventiveness in the ordering of our lives. We are also aware that many of the things we have which seem to the Europeans to be luxuries are actually necessities, in the terms of our life. For this reason, we are not fully able to respect the sources of this envy on the part of others.

We observe, furthermore, that people are inclined to identify us with tendencies in their own society which they do not like—ones which arise from purely domestic causes, and which would be there whether we Americans existed or not. We suspect that we are often the scapegoats, generally, for Europe's own inability to resist such things as industrialism, mass culture, overpopulation, the decline of good living, the vulgarization of taste. Plainly, it is easier to attribute these evils to us, and to picture oneself as the innocent victim of external influence, than to recognize them as indigenous phenomena. We feel that very often we are disliked, not wholly for our own sakes, but simply because the European fears the American in himself.

For that inner American that inhabits the English and European breast, we must again disclaim all responsibility.

It is not our influence that is causing you to choke your highways and jeopardize the integrity of your communities by the headlong introduction of the automobile. There is nothing that requires you to drink our soft drinks, to dance to our music, to view our motion pictures, or to drug your children with comic books. There will be, I assure you, no serious international repercussions if you reject these things.

Finally, before we Americans get carried away with a sense of guilt, we have to ask ourselves whether things could really have been expected to be any different from what they are. This is rather important; for if the answer is "no," then our condition is no fit subject for resentment. When I see people in Europe indignant over the way we behave, I am moved to reflect that the way we behave is—when you stop to think of it—exactly the way one hundred and sixty million Europeans, or their descendants, would behave if they were to be put over into the New World and subjected to the influences, and the discipline of experience, that we have been subjected to. This, in fact, is precisely what has happened. When the European sees us as we are today, he ought really to say: "There, but for the grace of God, go I!" for it is only fortune, the merit, perhaps, of his forefathers but no merit of his, that has saved him from this fate.

I think I hear already the reply that will be made by some of my English friends to these considerations. "Irritating as you sometimes are, individually," it will be said, "it is not your personal idiosyncrasies that give us the most concern;

these things are relatively unimportant; it is the policies of your government that we really object to. It is for your behavior collectively, not as individuals, that you are most unpopular."

This is, of course, a very serious matter. It would be idle to deny the depth and the gravity of the issues over which our governments have, on occasions, tended to disagree. I am not a spokesman for my own government; and I did not come here to debate these issues on its behalf. But there are one or two things I should like to observe in this connection which do not always seem to be taken into account on this side of the water.

First of all, these issues you have in mind are, without exception, I believe, ones on which Americans themselves are widely divided. This may be small comfort to you; but it would, one would think, imply a certain obligation to avoid generalization. The Americans are not marching on you in a solid phalanx under the banner of anti-colonialism or racial prejudice or the defense of Chiang Kai-shek. One cannot, therefore, assume of the individual private American acquaintance that he bears personal responsibility for all these manifestations of the American official mind which are least congenial to people elsewhere.

We ought further to recognize, I think, that most of these issues which divide us are very complex ones indeed, in which there is usually something to be said for both sides of the argument. Both our governments may take positions that meet with the sharpest rejection on the other side of the water; but surely never are they taken for that specific purpose. When one looks a little deeper, one sees that there are always reasons—and usually serious, respectable ones—why these particular positions are taken, despite their unpopularity abroad. Nor are the alternatives to them always necessarily ideal, or the arguments against them 100 per cent sound.

There are those of us in America, for example, who have deplored as much as anyone in England what we hold to have been our government's extravagant commitment to the Chinese Nationalists; yet we have felt that some of our allies in the recent war in the Pacific have shown themselves a bit obtuse from time to time to the danger of letting the Communists get hold of the great workshop of Japan, and that we might have expected a bit more sympathy and understanding in the efforts we ourselves have made to this end, including the effort to prevent Formosa from becoming a Russian air and naval base. There are those of us who deeply admire some of the British achievements in colonial administration, and have only contempt for the demagogic denunciations of colonialism that emanate from the Communist camp; yet we know that there is such a thing as clinging too long to a colonial relationship that has lost its rationale, and we have seen instances where this has brought much trouble and embarrassment to the Western community at large. There are some of us in the United States who promptly and publicly condemned the stand our government took in the Suez matter; yet most of us who did this would not wish it to be assumed, I am sure, that this condemnation implied an enthusiasm for the manner in which the matter was handled by the other governments involved. There are many of us, finally, to whom every report of racial intolerance in our country is like the stab of a knife, for we know what failure to solve this problem can do to our country; yet we cannot identify ourselves with the smug superiority of the European who finds it easy to be tolerant toward the colored minority he does not have.

These are all tangled problems. None of our positions is apt to be wholly devoid of merit, yet none, by the same token, is apt to be without fault. Perhaps we should all remind ourselves, from time to time, of that celebrated plea which is now a part of our common history: "I beseech you, in the bowels of Christ, think it possible you may be mistaken." It was, if I remember correctly, an Englishman who spoke these words—and other Englishmen to whom he spoke them.

I cannot see that anything will be gained by trying to convince ourselves that the present sources of our differences are going to get better at any early date. I see no reason to suppose that we will irritate you any the less ten years hence than we do now. You will continue for a long time to have need of us as the scapegoats for things you do not like in yourselves. We will continue to see world affairs differently

from you, if only for the reason that our geographical position, our needs, and our perspective are all different from
yours.

And despite the fact that the entertainment industry
tends to bring you and ourselves closer together, I doubt
that we are destined to become with the course of time more
and more alike. This is particularly true when it comes to
the realm of public life. The drying up of the stream of
immigration from Europe—once the greatest of cultural
bonds between the old country and the new—is now tending to strengthen and confirm all that is specific in our
society. We are becoming not less American, but more so.
And the shift of the political center of gravity in America
that is now in progress—the shift from the more cosmo-
politan Eastern seaboard to such places as Texas and Cali-
fornia—means that the people who predominate in our
public life are in the nature of things going to be, in future,
ones less accustomed to your ways, less familiar with your
problems, and endowed with less detachment toward themselves, than those who dealt with Anglo-American affairs at,
say, the turn of the century.

In these circumstances, I see only two things that will
really help us. The first is the absence of sentimentality.
The time has passed, if it ever existed, when we could help
ourselves very much with hopeful references to the Magna
Charta, and with a glossing over of our real difficulties. A
great deal has occurred since the time when a tiny group of

rather unrepresentative Englishmen crossed the water so uncomfortably in the good ship *Mayflower*; and it is no good laboring the significance of that event as a palliative for our present differences.

Frankness is what we need—frankness, if need be, to the point of brutality. I have often thought, observing our contacts at the official level, that you British, being a polite race, make the mistake of being too nice to us. We see and appreciate the effort made to avoid giving offense, to say the pleasant thing, and to appeal to our prejudices. But also we sense the undercurrent of suppressed exasperation on which this delicacy is so often borne. You would do better, if I may say so, to tell us bluntly what you think of us, and to explain, patiently and insistently, why you think we are wrong. Our shoulders are broad. We can take it.

That is the first of the two requirements. The other is that we overcome the tendency to view what transpires on the other side of the water as something external to ourselves—as a drama the outcome of which does not concern us—a game in which we have no stake.

One sometimes gets the impression that many English people think that we Americans have no real problems at all; or that, to the extent they exist, they are ones an Englishman can observe with amused detachment. Conversely, there are plenty of Americans who could not know less or care less about the issues that agitate British public life. In both instances, this is a very shortsighted outlook.

What are the things we worry about in my own country?

There are many of them. It is hard to find any logical order to put them in. We worry over all the characteristic phenomena of industrialism and urbanization. We worry about what the machine does to man—about what becomes of creativity and imagination and the sense of independent achievement in the man who works at the lathe. We worry about what is happening to our great urban areas—about the disintegration of our cities as communities under the impact of the automobile. We worry about our youth—about the depression of educational standards through the huge new influx of children, far more than we can cope with, into our schools. We worry about the effects of television and passive recreation of all kinds on the minds of young people, and on their capacity for creative enjoyment. We worry about the juvenile delinquency in our great cities; about what happens to the child when both parents work and he is left to seek companionship and appreciation and the sense of adventure in the life of the streets. We worry, in the case of our older student generation, about what seems to us to be their exaggerated demand for security, their lack of the spirit of adventure—even of protest —their interest in knowledge for utilitarian purposes rather than for its own sake. Some of us worry, finally, about the phenomenon of "bigness" in government: about this appalling proliferation of bureaucracy, and what it does to government itself; to the ease of communication within it, to the capacity for insight, the inciseness of decision, the humanity of approach, and the style of leadership.

We worry about the creeping inflation that has characterized our economy ever since the crisis; and we puzzle as to how we can combine a system in which no one needs to work at a job he doesn't like with the financial discipline requisite to protecting the savings of a growing population of old people, pensioners and people on fixed incomes. We worry about finding the right proportion between the amount of our national product to devote to defense against outside encroachment, and the amount that is to go into the normal development of our economy. We worry about the exhaustion of our natural resources and the blighting of our landscape by the headlong industrialization on which we are embarked. We worry, finally, and a great deal in fact, about our color problem, which has torn our life into pieces once, and can do so again.

Are these issues wholly foreign to British life? Some more so, some less so, no doubt; but none so much so, surely, that anyone here can really be indifferent to the manner in which they are resolved on our side of the water.

And conversely: do you suppose that you English have a monopoly on the foreign-political difficulties that beset you? Can you assume for one instant that your international position of today is essentially different from what ours is becoming?

Let us not exaggerate the difference between sixty million

people and a hundred and sixty million in the face of the enormous and growing populations of Asia and Africa. We Americans already represent, like yourselves, a small, privileged minority in an overcrowded world. We, too, are faced with the task of defending a high standard of living and all the luxuries of a permissive society against the jealousies and resentments of countless millions who are just awakening to an awareness of world affairs, and who would witness without pity or regret the disappearance of much that we value. Like yourselves, we are becoming increasingly dependent on the resources of this jealous outside world for the maintenance of our life; and we, like you, can be and will be put to cruel choices, on occasions, to know how to reconcile this dependence with our basic good will and our desire to live at peace with all peoples. We, too, are an island, in our way, confined by our two oceans as you are by your seas; and the effect of modern technology has been to make our country smaller, quicker to cross, and more closely knit psychologically, than was the England of very recent memory.

Is there, by chance, an impression here that whereas England's star is on the decline, we Americans are a dynamic, coming nation, lucky beyond our deserts, riding the wave of the future, moving into the glories of world dominion? To judge by recent trends, this is hardly the case. We are rapidly becoming a highly conservative welfare state, psychologically sufficient unto ourselves, largely committed—

as I have just suggested—to the maintenance of over-employment in the name of social security, to a creeping inflation which we seem to have no serious intention of combating, to a growing dependence on the resources of others, and to the cultivation of a comfortable life at home. This, whatever else it may be, is not the imperial frame of mind. If it were true, which I think it is not, that all this that we see around us here in England could properly be called decadence, then ours would be the decadence of tomorrow, no less tragic, no less deepseated.

Personally, I do not believe in this thesis of decadence; I think there are still great sources of strength in both peoples, of which we ourselves are poorly conscious and about which the non-European world knows nothing. But whatever our strength, whatever our weaknesses, your paths and ours are much the same. In some respects, you move in our footsteps; in others, we move in yours.

What folly, in the light of these reflections, to suppose that we might have anything to gain from your reverses, or you from ours. On the contrary, when your city planners win a battle in the struggle against urban blight, we are the gainers. When you discover, within the unique framework of your Commonwealth, some means of ordering your relationships with distant peoples that obviates this tension between the developed and the underdeveloped and promises fruitful collaboration and confidence, the victory is ours as well as yours. When we discover means of bringing the delinquent juvenile back to a sense of belonging and security in the world he finds before him, of satisfying his sense of adventure and reconciling him with home and society, it is your Teddy boys, as well as ours, who are helped. I daresay that even when one of our communities comes out on the side of tolerance and maturity in this most miserable and agonizing of all struggles, the ordering of the relationship between blacks and whites (and many of them do; it is only the unsuccessful ones you hear about), you British are helped, whether you know it or not, and your world, too, is made that much easier to live in.

I am not saying that things are going well on both sides of the water, in all these respects. I am not prophesying that the forces of decency and enlightenment are always going to win. I don't know what the outcome of many of these issues is going to be in my own country. Some of them now hang in the balance. We Americans too have our ups and downs. We have all gone through moments of discouragement; and again we have often been rebuked for that discouragement by the native resourcefulness and good sense our people tend to manifest whenever the issues present themselves in their ultimate form. It is usually when one is about to despair of Americans that they suddenly show their greatest qualities. But I do not, as I say, know what the future is going to bring. I cannot promise that what you would regard as the forces of virtue and righteousness in our life will always win out. And whether they do or not is beside my point.

I wish only to demonstrate that life in America is a great struggle among the characteristic forces of the modern age, and that you, whether you like it or not, are parties to this struggle. You are not alone in your distaste for certain American phenomena. You have millions of allies in these feelings, among Americans themselves. Nor are these phenomena in any way exclusively American. Let us recognize our bond and move forward together against ostentation and vulgarity and intolerance wherever these things are to be found, not charging each other with their authorship but accepting them as a common problem.

So much for the over-all picture of Anglo-American relations.

I have purposely said nothing here about that little band of people, of whom I count myself a member, who know both countries, and who love them both, who have their friends in both, and who cannot conceive of a world in which both did not figure. I have left these people out of the discussion because they are not very numerous, because they do not wield much influence, and because I wish to obey my own injunction to avoid sentimentality.

Still, it is perhaps permissible to note, in concluding these talks, that such people do still exist, on both sides of the Atlantic. They do reinforce in a modest way the mortar of common interest and common danger by which the structure of Anglo-American solidarity must, in the main, be bound. Their position is not always an easy one; but they find unique and abiding satisfaction in it, and not for one instant would they exchange it for any other. That they still carry on—that they are still tolerated in this post-Suez era—that one of them, who is an American, should in fact be permitted to speak to a British audience as I have spoken to you on these occasions—is testimony to the fact that our mutual relationship has resources deeper than any of us can fathom, and so moving that one hesitates to make them the subject of any further words.